Teaching Notes

for piano examination pieces
Initial–Grade 8

Complete syllabus
2009–2011

Published by:
Trinity College London
89 Albert Embankment
London SE1 7TP UK

T +44 (0)20 7820 6100
F +44 (0)20 7820 6161
E music@trinityguildhall.co.uk
www.trinityguildhall.co.uk

Introduction

These notes have been prepared for the benefit of teachers and students preparing for piano examinations using the 2009-2011 syllabus. There is of course no 'one' way to play any piece of music, and this holds good for examinations just as much as for concert performances. Examiners will always be ready to accept many different ways of playing the pieces, so long as they are well prepared, carefully thought out and appropriate for the style of the music being performed.

From Initial to Grade 3 there is one list of pieces only, from which three pieces are freely chosen. From Grade 4 up to Grade 8 pieces are in two groups; two pieces are chosen from one group and one from the other. This arrangement allows candidates to play as much as possible of the music that they themselves enjoy and which shows off their skills in the best and most balanced way. As with all examination programmes, candidates should aim to demonstrate a variety of styles and techniques within their programme.

Marks are awarded separately to each piece for each of three main areas:

- Notational accuracy & fluency: how well the notes are prepared and delivered. More conveniently thought of as: 'Me and the Music'.

- Technical facility: instrumental control and the ability to draw the most from the instrument; tone colour, articulation, pedalling etc.: 'Me and the Instrument'.

- Communication and interpretation: how well candidates give their performance, engage the audience and convey a sense of the meaning of the music they are playing: 'Me and the Audience'.

Detailed criteria for assessing each performance are published, and candidates and teachers should look carefully at those that relate to the grade being taken to make sure that their preparation is correctly focused.

A final word of advice: enjoy practising and performing the pieces – your enjoyment will come across to the examiner and it will make the examination a happier event for everyone involved.

Teachers may photocopy pages from this book to use with students; it may be helpful to enlarge the copy.

Where publisher details are given as Trinity Guildhall this indicates that the piece is included in the piano book for the grade.

Entry Level

At Entry Level (Initial), candidates will typically be able to show that they have acquired a basic foundation on their instrument; they will demonstrate some interpretation through variation in dynamics and articulation, with a limited variety of pace. They will perform audibly, with a sense of enthusiasm and enjoyment and with some awareness of audience. These features will be demonstrated through material that is short enough to allow candidates at this level to maintain concentration through to the end. Content will be simple and straightforward, often with attractive titles relating to familiar subjects and contexts. The musical language will be simple and accessible.

Initial

Alexander	The Merry Merry-Go-Round	Trinity Guildhall

Just as the horses rise and fall on the merry-go-round, so Alexander's tune falls into the bass clef and then climbs back into the right hand's territory. Careful listening will ensure a perfect *legato* and match of sound between the hands. In the central section the composer asks for an exaggerated contrast between the strong, *legato* melodic line and the light, *staccato* accompanying chords – difficult when they happen at the same time! It's good for pianists to understand the differing physical sensations for these touches early on, and achieving them at the same time is a wonderful coordination exercise.

Not the most musically challenging piece, but it covers useful and important technical issues.

Carroll	May Day Dance	Trinity Guildhall

Originally all the pieces in Walter Carroll's *Scenes at a Farm* had accompanying verses – an excellent way of getting pianists to understand that phrases have shape, places of tension and places of relaxation. Imagine ending the first phrase with a question mark, then answering the question and resolving the tension in the second phrase. No repeat in the exam, so you are quickly launched into the ensuing *f* to *p* exchange: arm-weight is needed for the accents and gentle but precise fingerwork for the crotchet melody. The four-bar *Coda* is the only place where the hands move from a five-finger position. Find a way to draw a vibrant, ringing sound out of the piano here.

Gruber	The Acrobat	Trinity Guildhall

The acrobat confidently hops between the black and white notes in this quirky piece. Perhaps one to teach by rote. It is rather like 'chopsticks' in the way that, for most young children, it will be far easier to learn kinaesthetically, by copying and remembering the physical movements, than it will be to read. The added dynamics are editorial and slipping back to a *mp* again just for bar 10, where the hands briefly return to the white notes, is an attractive option.

Straightforward and fun – well worth learning whether or not it is chosen for the exam!

| Hall | In the Desert | Trinity Guildhall |

In so many of her pieces Pauline Hall manages to combine sound pedagogical writing with immediate appeal – and this one is no exception. The desert setting conjures pictures of camels, swinging gently from side to side as they unhurriedly traipse across the sand. Use this image to encourage a quiet, steady rotary movement in the left hand. The obligatory Arabic-sounding augmented second may be an awkward stretch for very small hands, and if it feels uncomfortable it will probably sound it, so adjust the fingering if necessary. As the camels come closer the volume of the melody increases, then gradually dies away as they lumber off into the distance.

Musically sophisticated and rather haunting. Use the repetitive left hand as a strong selling point.

| McNeill | Play Party [duet part optional] | Trinity Guildhall |

A bright, cheerful piece, full of articulation detail. Also an ideal opportunity to work on the 'drop-float' technique for these two-note slurs: the hand drops on to the first note then, as the wrist rises to release the note, the second note is played almost passively. When the hands play together it feels comfortable to match the fingering, and you may like to bear this in mind for the contrary motion bars in the central section, using the same fingering for each bar (fingers 2, 3 and 4) and moving the hand for each position change. It sounds complicated, but it works extremely well! The lack of slur in bar 16 is ambiguous: does the composer mean us to separate these notes, or did she simply forget to add the slur? It is good for pianists to know there are some interpretative decisions they need to make themselves.

| Milne | Spiral Staircase | Trinity Guildhall |

Played at the top metronome speed, this must be one of the shortest examination pieces ever! Once you know exactly where the hands are going – it moves around quite a bit – it is enormous fun to play and the problem will be making sure that pianists don't get faster and faster. Probably best with a wrist *staccato*, feeling the difference in drop between the *mf* and *mp*, with arm added for the *f* at the end. Find the hidden scales in the first eight bars to make it easier to learn. Teachers may like to play it 'badly' to their students, getting them to call out when notes stick out, or the hand changes are too audible or the pulse unsteady. If students can hear other people's mistakes, they are more likely to listen out for their own.

| Scher | Mr Oom Pah | Trinity Guildhall |

The title, linked to the steady tempo, brings tubas and trombones to mind. It probably refers to the alternating *staccato* chords in the third and fourth lines, but that cheeky slide from G to Ab in bar 12 is surely made by a mischievous brass player. Good to see the odd snippet of melody in the left hand, although combining differing articulations in each hand will make this a more challenging choice. Teachers could try first to get pianists playing simple five-note exercises *staccato* in one hand and *legato* in the other. Brilliant for coordination and, it is said, for getting both sides of the brain to work in harmony.

Watts	Wondering, pondering	Trinity Guildhall

The chromaticism in the harmony adds an air of poignancy to this touching piece and the melody, fitting neatly into a five-finger position, seems to turn round on itself, just like turning thoughts over in your head. Although not specified, surely the right hand should be played with a fluid, singing *legato*, whilst the left hand keeps a supple wrist to avoid any clunking on the repeated chords. Many smaller hands may find it easier to use a thumb on the G#/Ab, and this may also avoid the thumb and little finger sitting too near the edge of the keys. Beginning firmly enough will leave plenty of room to show the contrast in the second half.

Wedgwood	Whirleybird	Trinity Guildhall

Wedgwood has chosen an F five-finger position for her waltz, with small extensions in the left hand only. The repetition means that there are actually very few bars to learn, but fine judgment is needed in matters of touch to achieve the different dynamic levels demanded on each line. Of course this can be approached purely physically, but it may also be helpful to think of singing these same notes in different moods: wistful, defiant, shy or carefree perhaps? Or imagine them being played by different instruments: clarinet, trumpet, flute and violin for instance.

Foundation Level

At Foundation level (Grades 1-3), candidates will typically be able to apply their knowledge, understanding and skills to produce a performance that demonstrates careful preparation, understanding and the beginning of thoughtful interpretation based on some creative engagement with the material. Candidates will perform clearly and accurately, with a fluent technical command appropriate to the level and a sense of spontaneity, sustaining these qualities through to the end. Through variations in pace, volume, rhythm and articulation they will be able to create and convey mood. These features will be demonstrated through material of sufficient length to allow candidates to show their ability to establish and sustain their performance and interpretation. Content will include easily recognisable styles (e.g. minuet, blues) as the foundation for the exploration of musical styles outside their immediate experience. The musical language will contain a variety of expression across the three pieces and will demand awareness of balance and phrase.

Grade 1

Hook	Minuetto	Trinity Guildhall

Many of the early grade minuets, jigs and waltzes can sound a little formulaic, but there is something very satisfying about the symmetry and balance in pieces such as this Minuetto by Hook. The dotted rhythms in the right hand need to be crisp but not bumpy – play the semiquaver exactly in time, but without an accent. Although that is not easy to achieve, at least you will soon notice that the third and fourth lines are almost the same as lines one and two!

Pianists will probably have come across two-note slurs before, but here they join chords in thirds. The same principles apply, but more involvement of arm-weight will be needed. Synchronisation can sometimes be an issue in thirds, particularly when there are black notes involved. It may help to make sure that the fingers are lightly resting on the surface of the keys before the notes are played. Many of the comments for the following Mozart Minuet apply here too. It will be difficult to choose between them, but useful for teachers to have the two of them side by side to point out their similarities.

Mozart	Minuet, K. 6	Trinity Guildhall

There was a Mozart Menuett in the last syllabus and it seems that he wrote these whilst still a boy as exercises to practise various chord progressions. Many composers could have used the same chords in the first bars, and would probably have suspended the C over the G harmony in bar 2, but Mozart colours this suspension by raising it to C♯ and then resolves it upwards. He also avoids strong downbeats in the bass, practically subverting the whole idea of a minuet. Is it hindsight that leads us to see these and other elements as evidence of an unusual musical sophistication?

The two-note slurs in both hands ask for graceful phrasing in both dynamic and articulation. Listen to the sound of the minims in the final bars of each section (originally appoggiaturas) and try to match the resolution to the decay of the previous note. Where there are no markings for the bass line the notes can be slightly detached, always bearing in mind the implied stresses of the dance. The suggested dynamics are good, but not obligatory; you may want to find a more intimate shading for the return to the tonic key in bars 11-12.

Gurlitt	Morning Greeting	Trinity Guildhall

This must be a Sunday morning – relaxed and easy-going, with just a hint of excitement for the day ahead on the third line. In bars 1, 2, 5 and 6 the left-hand chords will release with the end of the slur in the right hand, but note that when their roles change, the accompanying right-hand chords need to sustain right until the end of the bar. It is tricky not to bump the third note in the slurs. Try to feel that the three notes are being played from one impulse – rather like saying 'likeable', where the word has a natural *diminuendo*. Gurlitt is also asking rather a lot to have a *crescendo* from *mf* to *f* over three long bars; Imagine that each individual bar is shaped away from the downbeat, so the bars as units get louder, rather than getting louder through each bar. No sentimentality is needed at the end of this early morning piece, so try to avoid getting slower in the final bars.

Rowley	Ill Temper	Trinity Guildhall

The mood is all here: you need to remember what it feels like to be in a bad mood, then find a way of projecting that feeling, without getting so carried away that you lose control. The key to this is probably going to be a crisp, firm *staccato* with the ends of slurs losing all pretence of their usual passive, polite fading away. Firm fingers, yes, and arm weight on the chords, but within reason – no bashing at the *ff*. The final *stringendo* will work best if you come down a notch in dynamic to allow room to explode on the final chord.

Plenty of confidence needed here, but keep a cool head to avoid splitting notes or making an ugly sound.

Shostakovich	Waltz	Trinity Guildhall

This will not be an easy option but, Shostakovich has written an absolute jewel, within its limited technical constraints. He begins traditionally, with balanced, classical phrasing and a typical waltz style (be on the lookout for pianists who forget to detach the second and third left-hand crotchets in bars 2, 4 etc.). The first half is gently melancholic, but it is in the ensuing section that Shostakovich undermines this careful classicism, suddenly slipping from A minor into a world of flats, taking us 'through the looking glass'. On the last line the intervals seem too small, as though the music is being gently squeezed through the bottleneck, back out into the calm mood of A minor. The ending is understated; our adventures will remain a secret. A singing, flowing *legato* is needed for the melody – flexible wrists and sensitive fingertips to make the phrasing sound natural and effortless.

A challenging but worthwhile choice.

York	A Legend	Trinity Guildhall

The hands swap roles in this sad piece, but there is always a clear divide between foreground and background. So if the general dynamic asked for is *mf*, this will need to be achieved with a subtle combination of a shade below that level in the chordal accompaniment and a shade above it in the melody. Getting pianists to play five-finger exercises or scales with one hand louder than the other is good practice for this (and for brain coordination). If they find that difficult, get them to play one hand just after the other first; e.g. left hand plays the first note softly, followed by right hand playing the same note an octave higher loudly, etc. Gradually the two notes can be played closer together, until they are being played simultaneously – hopefully with one hand still playing louder than the other! York's dynamic markings are precise and demanding, and words may also be a clue to getting the phrasing. 'There was a princess. She lived alone … but', may help the first phrase shape the *diminuendo*, but the second feel as though it is going forward. The final sighs can be very affecting; make sure we really do hear the brief silence after each pair of notes.

Haughton	The Secret Garden	Trinity Guildhall

This is a modest gem; beautifully crafted with great charm and wistfulness. There is an implied waltz phrasing in bars 2, 4, 6 etc. – keep a lightness of touch and articulation in the second and third crotchets, ensuring that the right-hand fifth finger is not collapsing on to its side and that the left-hand thumb plays with discretion! As the child goes further into the garden, the music flirts with the tonic minor coloured by hints of the Neapolitan, until a small *crescendo* – the only time the dynamic rises above piano – returns us to the opening melody. Silence, that empty bar just before the end, is often difficult to hold. Try getting students to echo the previous bar in their heads rather than simply counting to three. Or perhaps get them to feel the tension in the air left by the previous unanswered phrase and judge the right moment shyly to provide the answer.

This one is for those with sensitive souls.

Chapple	Keeping Busy	Trinity Guildhall

Some tricky right-hand chords to learn here, but the left hand is wonderfully straightforward and the upbeat, energetic mood will attract many. The whole of the left hand can be played in one position until the very last bar, although small hands may find it more comfortable to begin on a thumb and give the fourth finger a workout for the first three lines. If you opt for the printed fingering, check that the fifth finger is well-supported for the accents – no karate chops! The chords in bars 13–16 will be most easily learnt if initially played as sixths descending by semitones. Once that is assimilated, change the second chord's top note – easy! Similar strategies can be used earlier on, perhaps learning those awkward thirds without the chromatic alterations first. Playing games with pieces can often lead to a greater sense of flexibility and understanding about how the notes were actually chosen. It can also get pianists to lose that fear of the wrong note which, paradoxically, can often lead to tension in the playing and the sound. A succession of 'will she, won't she' offbeat accents lead to a smiling, discreet exit.

Mier	Just Struttin' Along	Trinity Guildhall

This is bound to be chosen by many pianists for its easy-going jazzy style, but it is far from easy to play well. Fortunately there are not so many notes to learn as Mier repeats the same material in the second half of the piece. The 'swung' rhythm will need to be absolutely precise so as not to lose the effect of the rests in the first and last four bars and the quavers here should probably be slightly separated to contrast with the marked *legato* elsewhere. The octave shifts up and down the piano are made even more challenging by the meticulous dynamic markings. Try getting students to move two octaves away, and then one octave will feel much easier. Notice too, the difference between bar 5, when the last melody note needs to be held to the end of the bar, and bars 6 and 7, where the last note must be immediately released so that it doesn't overlap into the next bar.

Telemann	Rigaudon (from *Piano All Sorts* Initial-Grade 1)	Trinity Faber

Born only four years before J S Bach, Georg Philipp Telemann was generally more highly regarded by contemporaries than his younger friend. He studied languages and science, meanwhile teaching himself to play a variety of instruments, including the zither and shawm! This Rigaudon is fairly typical of the baroque dances used for teaching. It is strictly in two parts and, although the left hand plays a supporting role, it will nonetheless need shaping. Look out for places where it moves in contrary or similar motion with the right hand – they will make the hands-together learning seem less daunting. As usual, some articulation will need to be added, perhaps a lightly detached upbeat to show the start of each new phrase. The *tempo giusto* (in strict time) marking is editorial, but it is good advice for this rather earthy dance.

J C F Bach	Menuet (from *At the Piano with the Sons of Bach*)	Alfred

Johann Christoph Friedrich was Johann Sebastian's sixteenth child – not to be confused with Johann Christoph, who was J S's uncle, or Johann Christian, another son! They were all professional musicians, but J C F is probably the least known of these four Johanns. This Menuet is relatively straightforward. The left hand has no phrasing marked, so try allowing it to follow that of the right hand. Ask students to experiment with the articulation in the last bar of each section – all *staccato*? two-note slur then *staccato*? There is a good deal of movement around the keyboard and to begin with it will not be easy to read and find the right notes as well as getting the rhythm and articulation correct. It may be useful to use some rote learning here, working in small phrases, so that reading the music is not an issue. All changes of position need to be thoroughly practised, always keeping a flexible wrist, so that they flow easily and are set firmly in the muscular memory.

Gurlitt	Presto (no. 18 from *Les études poco forte – The Pianist's Repertory*)	Lemoine

At first glance this is not too inspiring: composed almost entirely of tonics and dominants, with a brief modulation to the dominant in the middle. But this lack of originality should make it all the more easy to learn and then students can concentrate on working it up to a good *presto* tempo – it should finally sound quite impressive! *Legato* broken chords are standard fare; the suggested fingering is less common than beginning with 135 and either would be perfectly acceptable. Keep the wrists supple and avoid accenting the thumb on each beat – it may help to imagine a small *crescendo* through these bars. The *diminuendo* in bar 11 can be quite pronounced, allowing a good build-up to a strong, triumphant ending. Not many subtleties here, but it could become a favourite!

| Bartók | Where Have You Been, Little Lamb? | |
| | (from *First Term at the Piano*) | EMB |

This evocative title conjures up biscuit-tin images of rural peace and simplicity and Béla Bartók's gentle accompaniment does nothing to disturb this tranquillity. The melody was originally sung, so concentrate on producing a warm, *cantabile* tone in the right hand. Either hand can take the Ds in bars 7 and 8, as long as the integrity of the melody is not lost. There is no need to add dynamic contrasts to the repeated phrases. Adults often forget how enjoyable repetition can be for children; this folk song, like *London's Burning* or *Frère Jacques* exploits that. The left hand will need support from the arm, both to balance the chords comfortably in the first section and to achieve a relaxed rotary motion in the second. Practise this rocking movement initially without worrying about the correct notes and then be sure that students understand where the movement changes to accommodate the stepwise contrary motion passages between the hands.

| Járdányi | Hoppity Hop (from *Piano All Sorts* Initial-Grade 1) | Trinity Faber |

This unusual piece needs a really strong pulse and a sense of drama as the raucous fifths interrupt the gently hopping theme. Either through playing the piece to students, or by clapping or singing it with them, help them understand the rhythmic character and the uneven shape of the phrases before they start to learn the notes. They will soon be able to make up a story to go with the music and this will add an extra dimension to their performance. The changes of dynamic need to be sudden and dramatic, particularly in bar 20 – imagine a cut in a film to an entirely different scene. For the repeated fifths, try lowering the wrist on the crotchet and gradually raising it on the two (or three) quavers. This should avoid too rough a sound. A firm, decisive ending is needed, so use strong fingers for those last two notes. Above all, have fun with this one!

| Last | The Lonely Track | |
| | (from *By Land and Sea: The Essential Joan Last*) | Stainer & Bell |

Pieces like this show just why Joan Last was such a popular composer, both for teachers and students. It is packed with musical detail, so there is plenty here to fire the imagination. Students could make up their own story of what happens on this lonely track, ensuring that all the dynamic detail fits into their interpretation. The details also provide many opportunities to revise various technical issues. The phrasing is important: not all phrases begin on the downbeat, and lines will need sensitive dynamic shaping and articulation to make this audible. Accents largely underpin the phrasing, emphasising perhaps the tiredness of this walker. A little extra arm weight on these, using a 'drop-float' action, but they do not need to be too exaggerated in this context. Places where the left hand echoes the right should be brought out, particularly at the very end, where the opening phrase returns at half speed. The *con expressione* is clearly a misprint, but an appropriate direction for this musically challenging choice.

| Milne | Chase (from *Very Easy Little Peppers*) | Faber |

Such a catchy tune from the author of all the *Little Peppers* books is bound to make this a favourite choice – especially as much of the second page is a repeat of the first. Elissa Milne makes sneaky changes though in the articulation that need to be noted. In the opening section she uses *staccato* and *tenuto* to emphasise the syncopation – lifting the first note in bar 2 helps to throw the stress on to the second. But when the same rhythm returns in the middle section, all is *legato*. She also modifies the first crotchets of each phrase: at first they are marked *tenuto*, but later they also have *staccato* dots. In both cases they need to be weighted, but will be slightly more detached (not a real *staccato*) in the second instance. The gradual *crescendo* throughout the middle section will only work if pianists come right down to p in bar 9. A firm, well-supported little finger is needed for the accent on the very last note – no collapsing here – and an agitated mood and tempo will help interpret the title.

Wedgwood	Damsel in Distress (from *Creepy Crawlies!*)	Trinity Faber

Pam Wedgwood's damsel in distress is a damsel fly – a clever play on words, and this enchanting music does not make the distress sound that severe! Right-hand quavers buzz in lazy circles; Wedgwood asks for them to be played lightly and it will take careful listening to ensure that no one finger (or thumb) sticks out and spoils the effect. The upbeat in the left hand would sound good detached and make sure that the following *mf* bars really do sound warmer and richer in tone. Hold the tie and the chord towards the end for their full length and get students to experiment with the last phrase: can they release the final As so slowly that the sound dies imperceptibly, or can they control the *diminuendo* so that the notes fade away on the pause?

Wood	Gigue (from *Piano Time Pieces* 2)	OUP

This is such a light-hearted piece – it is difficult to resist smiling while playing it! Of the pieces in compound time in the Grade 1 list this one, with such an uncomplicated, appealing tune, will be a good starting point for assimilating $\frac{6}{8}$ rhythms. Try asking students to tap a pulse with their left hand on the piano, or on their knee, while playing the right hand. This should be a useful prelude to adding the light, *staccato* bass to the *legato* melody. The initial five-finger position, with the fourth finger on B♭, is not the most comfortable: the hand will need to move into the keyboard so that the little finger can reach the C with ease and without falling on to its side! Start the final phrase more softly, so that the *crescendo* to the end is really effective.

Grade 2

Handel	Gavotte	Trinity Guildhall

This piece overflows with goodwill, but even a lively dance like the Gavotte still observes certain rules of poise and restraint that may not be easy for young pianists to relate to. Playing such a Gavotte today, or a Musette, or even a Minuet, is to travel through time, putting on the appropriate costumes and manners of the age. With so many period dramas on TV nowadays, perhaps these worlds are easier to enter than before, but getting students to listen to other Gavottes, and even look at fashion from the period, may help to set the tone.

The left hand notes can be lightly detached, and adding articulation to the right hand may also enhance the underlying character of the dance. Try releasing those first and third beat crotchets in bar 1 and elsewhere. Also note that dynamics are editorial; you may find the echoed second phrases too predictable and like to get students to make their own decisions. The bass line will cause most difficulties. Get pianists to play around with some of the patterns, the octave leaps, the I-V-I at cadence points, then learn the links between these. The hand seldom stays in one position for more than a few notes, so understanding why it leaps where it does will be important to help the memory.

Despréaux	Air: des trois fermiers	Trinity Guildhall

Few of us have heard of Monsieur Despréaux, but his dates (1748-1820) put him firmly into the Classical period. Born after Haydn and dying less than a decade before Beethoven, he looks back to the Baroque in the two-part writing of this Air, adding minor tinges to colour the more unusual central section.

Despréaux wrote this piece as part of a series of graded lessons designed to train pianists' fingers and introduce them to a variety of dances and popular tunes from opera and ballets. This air could well be one of the latter, sung or danced by three farmers. The music is not particularly bucolic – the emphasis seems to be on lyricism, on the 'aria' aspect, rather than anything more rustic. The phrase marks and dynamics are editorial and suggest long-term shaping, and the piece will come alive if this is audible. For instance, there is a clear summit to the first phrase in bar 2, with a relaxation as you approach the imperfect cadence. The phrase repeats, but this time the ending is more emphatic – a firm perfect cadence. So although the general dynamic is *mf*, there are ups and downs within this. This is an important interpretative point: dynamics are rarely blocks of sound, but rather reflect general mood and character.

Duvernoy	Study in F	Trinity Guildhall

Not all pieces titled 'Study' deserve the name, but this one does! Duvernoy is determined that we will understand the basics of waltz style: the accented downbeat and the light 'oom-pah-pah' accompaniment. And once you've successfully grasped those elements – and learnt the notes of course – then you are home and dry!

Quite often students need to be restrained from dropping on to the first notes of scales or other passage work, but here a gentle release of weight on to the first melody note of each bar, a drop after the preceding *staccato*, is just what is wanted for the accents. Notice the few bars that don't have accents, and try to make these sound different. Most of the study is within *p*, so keep the arms fairly light, supported at the shoulder. The left hand will be best learnt initially as chords; pieces like this, with their predictable, classical harmonic language, can be very useful for understanding and absorbing simple chord progressions. This study is rather repetitive, so try to play it towards the upper limit of the suggested metronome mark.

Koechlin　　　　Sicilienne　　　　　　　　　　　　　Trinity Guildhall

Charles Koechlin was a prolific French composer, writing many songs and piano pieces as well
as larger works for orchestra. He became involved in film music, often writing pieces inspired by
Hollywood. He trained with Massenet and Fauré at the Paris Conservatoire and, as with many French
composers of the time, colour became an important ingredient for him.

All siciliennes are gentle, swaying dances in compound time, often making use of the dotted rhythm
as Koechlin does here. Imagine different instruments playing this to encourage pianists to find more
colours. Perhaps a flute for the opening? Flatter fingers for that slightly breathy tone and a seamless
legato between the hands. Then the strings take over, with a solo viola enjoying its moment in the
limelight, playing with a warm vibrato, whilst the violins gently accompany. Bar 9 is tricky as the
notes of the violas and violins overlap in a way that is impossible to achieve on the piano without
sophisticated pedalling (not expected at this level). So don't be embarrassed about playing the first
right hand chord rather short and interrupting the left hand *legato* in the second half of the bar. The
penultimate bar is an awkward way of writing that the F♯ should be tied and held until the end of the
piece. The right hand simply takes over holding this note without replaying it.

A subtle piece that needs imaginative handling.

Goedicke　　　　Study no. 21　　　　　　　　　　　　Trinity Guildhall

Another study, but this time by a Russian composer and in a different style. Make the most of all
the details, particularly the difference between the accent in *p* in bar 4 and the same notes and
accent but this time within *f* at bar 20. The first needs just a small nudge, but the second is far more
dramatic, a really energised pluck with the fingers. Don't just think dynamic, think character: on the
first occasion those final two quavers nod their agreement, but the second time they vehemently
disagree, provoking a rather timidly placed B♭ in response – the first of the only two sustained
crotchets of the whole piece!

At *allegretto*, the tempo is not too challenging, rather giving performers plenty of time to show all
the detail. But the synchronisation in bars 3, 7 and elsewhere may deserve an exercise dedicated to
overcoming any problems it presents. Try playing one-octave scales beginning in this way, swapping
the hands around so that sometimes the right hand begins and the left hand joins a semiquaver later.
And the last chord – how many times do we play chords in precisely this position, a fifth apart in the
bass, a sixth in the right hand? Get students to practise it in a variety of keys to make finding this
ending secure.

Bartók　　　　Children's Song　　　　　　　　　　　Trinity Guildhall

The metronome mark is Bartók's, so these children must be in a thoughtful, quiet mood. This piece
comes from his first volume of *For Children*, in which all the pieces are based on Hungarian folk
tunes. A simple melody, eight balanced bars using only six notes, is transformed by Bartók's masterly
handling of harmony. He hints at other tonalities without actually settling in any of them, creating a
mood of idle wandering – or wondering – before the addition of the pedal on the last chords brings
a velvet warmth as the children find their way home. Dynamics are relative and are often more
successfully achieved if related to mood. Although it begins in *p*, there is still a sense of comfort,

of being at home in these first bars. If the sound is too tentative here, then it will be difficult to find something more tentative at the **pp**.

The right hand plays the melody three times, with only small additions or changes. Check that all the articulation is followed, perhaps adding your own words to help this. The left hand has the more awkward chords, and using arm-weight, making sure the arm is positioned behind the hand, will help synchronisation. The *legato* chords in bar 12-13 may sound better if the right hand helps out by taking the D of the third chord with its thumb.

Hindemith	Lied (song)	Trinity Guildhall

Let's build a Town, from where this *Lied* is taken, was an opera written for children, a model Britten would follow in his *Let's make an Opera*. There is a pleasing symmetry in the left-hand movement as it rolls from side to side, to the right for the thumb, then to the left for the little finger. This is a song to work to, with the pianist making the sort of rhythmic movements that seem to mimic the builder's craft.

The dynamics have been suggested by the editor, but a *crescendo* fits the middle section perfectly; as the bass gradually descends, the right hand adds notes and the tension increases. Perhaps the roof is being lifted into place? To make this work effectively, students will need to begin this long phrase fairly quietly, ensuring that the off-beat notes in the left hand don't project too loudly into the texture. It is a song, and the melody must remain in the spotlight. This balance may also need thought in the opening section: the melody should be phrased two bars at a time, whereas the accompaniment moves in much smaller units. Encourage students to sing the melody whilst doing the left-hand movements, first on the closed piano lid and then on the keyboard.

Bullard	Oxford Rag	Trinity Guildhall

This may be one of the few times that you will see 'with intelligence' as a performance direction. Combined with the title, it immediately makes us smile and puts us in the mood for this rather sophisticated rag. Students often find the syncopations in such pieces more natural than the style of a Mozart Minuet, but let them hear some of the Joplin rags, so that they can put this one in context.

The occasional left-hand slurs imply that elsewhere the crotchets should be detached. This is also true in the right hand, but here the quavers are best played *legato* – an interesting link with the baroque style, where we generally take a similar approach towards articulation, slurring shorter note values, and detaching longer ones. Get pianists to sing the tune whilst walking around the room to experience physically the syncopated rhythms against a steady pulse. There is a useful discussion to be had here about accidentals: which of them signify a change of key, and which are simply chromatic alterations? How can you tell the difference? Despite the *crescendos* and *f*s, the tone should not become hard or forced.

Kember	Song without Words	Trinity Guildhall

It was, of course, Mendelssohn who composed the most famous 'Songs without Words', but Kember's offering has a rather lovely, old-fashioned, melancholic charm. The jazz waltz, instead of repeating the second beat chord, sustains it, giving a sense of space in the middle of the bar, the suspension at the top of the circle. So the pulse is steady without being rigid; a dance, but one where the partners move gently together, probably holding each other closer than the typical arms' length waltz. Kember adds two *ralls* and pauses, further emphasising this flexibility.

The harmonies alternate between G major and A minor. Perhaps students could be helped to improvise around these keys, using the F♮ and G♯ to take them to A minor, then G♮ and F♯ to return them to G. The bass line is simple, but remarkably effective, as are the repeated snippets of melody over a descending bass line. Finding a good balance between singing melody, supportive bass notes and unobtrusive chords will be a challenge. Stress the need for pianists to listen carefully to their own sound, and check that all the joints in the arm stay supple – locked wrists or elbows will be detrimental to the tone.

Handel	March in G, HWV 419[3]	
	(no. 7 from *Handel Easy Piano Pieces and Dances*)	Bärenreiter

Bärenreiter give us a completely clean score, an *Urtext* edition, reproducing only what the composer wrote, although fingering suggestions have been added. Keyboard players of the period would have understood the stylistic conventions governing dynamics, articulation and phrasing, and teaching pieces such as these would have been used to pass on these traditions to their students. In this period, the beginning of the eighteenth century, people would have been using instruments like the harpsichord, which had a limited dynamic range. Nowadays it is accepted that on modern pianos dynamics are used as part of our means of expression.

This March has a strong, forthright character. Many of the crotchets, particularly those in the bass, could be played quite *staccato*, with *legato* quavers and slightly detached minims. Handel has asked for two, not four, beats in a bar, which implies a sense of forward direction and, although there is room for some dynamic variation – with either terraced or contrasting dynamics used on the repeated bars – the general level should be *f*. 'Ownership' is a popular word today, but allowing students to be involved in the musical choices in such a piece can also help them understand how important it is to follow the expression marks of other composers.

Petzold	Menuet in G minor, BWV Anh. 115	
(*attrib.* J S Bach)	from Notebook for Anna Magdalena Bach	
	(no. 2 from *Bach Easy Piano Pieces and Dances*)	Bärenreiter

This melancholy Menuet has usually been attributed to J S Bach, forming part of the Anna Magdalena Notebook. It is easy to see why: this is a well-crafted teaching piece, with enough distinctiveness to make its composition by a great master believable. Note that it was not so unusual to leave out the last flat in a minor key signature (this sixth note often needing to be sharpened during the piece) and that the direction *da capo* at the end should be ignored.

As in Handel's March above, Bärenreiter present a clean canvas. Some articulation needs to be added, for instance lightly detaching the second and third crotchets in bar 2; however the overall mood of this menuet seems to ask for a more lyrical approach. The downbeat stresses can be achieved through dynamics and phrasing instead, although lifting the last two crotchets in the penultimate bar of each section will be necessary to move to the final chords. The editorial suggestions for the mordents are good: at this stage they do not need to be too fast, but must be placed on the beat and not disturb the pulse.

Dussek	Minuet (from *Piano All Sorts* Grades 2-3)	Trinity Faber

Jan Ladislav Dussek was one of London's most celebrated pianists during his time there at the end of the eighteenth century, but is now, sadly, largely underrated. This was a golden age of pianism and the pianists, usually referred to as the London Pianoforte School, not only performed, but also composed and taught. Some, like Clementi, were also shrewd businessmen, becoming involved in publishing and piano manufacture. There is a wealth of excellent teaching material from that period, of which this dance is a good example.

Minuets abound in the early grade repertoire, but this one is particularly appealing. As always, the emphasis in each bar is on the first beat, but Dussek cleverly plays with the two-bar phrases, sometimes putting most importance on the first of two bars (bar 1), sometimes on the second (bar 4), and even having an equal stress on each (bars 5 and 6). This adds interest and life to the music, and performers need to show the phrasing through subtle dynamic shaping. There is an opportunity for neat rotary movement in the left hand in the middle section and where no *legato* is marked, use a lightly detached articulation on the crotchets.

Kuhlau	Andantino (from *Piano All Sorts* Grades 2-3)	Trinity Faber

This looks more difficult than it actually is. The key of B♭ major and the many chords may put off some teachers and students (although it is a set key for the grade). However it is both charming and ingenious. It is composed entirely on the tonic and dominant chords, yet manages to create enough variety of texture and mood to maintain musical interest. The repeat of the opening transposes phrases up or down the octave. This is a clever device, which Friedrich Kuhlau also uses in the understated *Coda*, and it is useful for encouraging free movement along the keyboard.

Given its limited harmonic range, it would be a good idea to spend some time finding and playing around with the chords of F^7 and B♭. Get students to play them in all inversions, to use them to make up accompaniments in various styles (waltz, march, '*alla* Moonlight sonata', etc.), to improvise melodies on top. In that way the left hand should then be easy to understand and learn. It is important to keep a singing melodic line at the forefront of the texture, even in the opening chords. Play the top line alone and then listen for clear projection of that voice when adding in the other parts. If it can be easily reached, a touch of pedal would help the last bars of each section.

| Gurlitt | Rocking Horse [with repeat] (no. 26 from | |
| | *Ponies – Easy Pieces with the Keyboard Crocodile)* | Breitkopf |

Horses are inevitably associated with $\frac{6}{8}$ and Cornelius Gurlitt's rocking horse is no exception. This is a very straightforward choice, not too challenging, with an almost exact repeat of the first section and a unison middle section. So the performance will need to be very good to gain high marks! A lively tempo, clean articulation and clear dynamic contrasts are required. At the right speed, the crotchets in bars 5–7 will be more or less *staccato*. The unison section bears a suspiciously strong resemblance to *God Rest Ye Merry Gentlemen*! The following link bars need careful timing to create a sense of suspense before, after a slight lift, the opening music returns.

| Bartók | Children at Play (from *Piano All Sorts* Grades 2–3) | Trinity Faber |

The two books of *For Children* have long been favourites with piano teachers as they are generally more immediately accessible to children than those in Béla Bartók's *Mikrokosmos* series. *Children at Play* is the first piece in the first volume, and is based on a Hungarian folk tune. It is a popular repertoire piece and ideal for work on articulation. Co-ordinating such different movements in each hand is supposed to be very good exercise for the brain and is also excellent preparation for other works by Bartók.

The 'drop-float' movement needs to be understood – two notes linked by one movement – even though here the second note falls on the beat and is sometimes marked to be stressed. The 23 fingering suggested for the string of two-note slurs in the left hand is ideal, as it insists that the hand lifts to change position for each. There is plenty of dynamic detail to observe, also demanding that the hands act independently. Finally, notice that the general dynamic level is gentle – not a boisterous piece this, but something quite simple and tender.

| Rockefeller | The Bubbling Brook (from *Jewels & Gems*) | Fischer |

No doubt about what this piece is practising, although it is a shame that the left hand does not also get a chance to play a chromatic scale. Instead, it rocks gently from side to side on tonic and dominant 7th chords. There is no choice about the fingering in the left hand, but you may prefer to modify the suggestions for the right, particularly in bar 12 (1 3 1 2 3 may suit some hands better). The dynamics basically follow a logical pattern of *crescendo* as the scale rises and *diminuendo* as it falls. Helen Rockefeller has tempered her *allegro* with *moderato*, so clean fingerwork should not be sacrificed for speed. A short *Coda* finishes this useful if rather predictable piece.

| Wedgwood | The Wonderful Wizard (from *Bewitched!*) | Trinity Faber |

How quickly fashions change. John Thompson's elves and Walter Carroll's fairies were replaced by frogs, dinosaurs and spaceships, and now, perhaps fuelled by J K Rowling's amazing success, we have wizards! There is nothing especially wizardly about this boogie-style piece, but if thoughts of Dumbledore or Gandalf inspire your students, that is all to the good!

The moving thumb in the left hand is typical of a boogie bass and also useful for developing flexibility in the thumb. Perhaps play around with splitting the chords, playing the left hand in a swing rhythm, which will also help develop a good rotary motion. Getting the syncopated rhythms in the right hand should be easy against such a strong bass, but watch out for bar 12, where there is suddenly no downbeat in the middle of the bar! The tempo is fairly steady, a strong pulse being more important than speed here, and contrasting dynamics are a feature and need good projection. Pam Wedgwood herself suggests making up words to the melody, so it could be useful that 'Harry Potter' neatly fits four swung quavers ...

York	Dopey Diplodocus (from *Dinosaurs!*)	Trinity Faber

John York may be a little behind fashion in preferring dinosaurs to wizards (see *The Wonderful Wizard* above), but there is so much inventive and pedagogically sound writing in this *Dopey Diplodocus*. Firstly there are the *tenuto* scrunched chords: a good opportunity to discuss and experiment with using arm weight. Then there are the two-note slurs, especially the glorious yawns with the semitone clashes between the hands: a good 'drop-float' action needed here. In this action the second note releases very lightly, the wrist rising after having dropped for the first note, the second note being struck quite passively. So the resultant sound will be much gentler than the active *staccato* required elsewhere in the piece.

Next comes the issue of playing a dancing, *cantabile* melody in the left hand, accompanied by the heavy dinosaur steps in the right – careful balancing needed here! Accents, commas (lift for a brief moment, as though the yawn interrupts the flow of the music), a final *rall.* as the dozey Dip drowses at the end ... all this detail makes for a marvellously imaginative piece. The final piece of inventiveness is that York calls the piece a minuet, reinventing this courtly dance for the twenty-first century dinosaur.

Grade 3

Kirnberger	Menuet	Trinity Guildhall

Kirnberger was a student of Bach's and, stylistically, this Menuet seems to lie somewhere between the minuets of Bach and Mozart. It uses two-part writing throughout, but the bass mostly describes the harmony, occasionally having small melodic links between phrases. The structure is unusual: a binary form, but each section is repeated with a decorated right hand. Kirnberger was primarily a violinist, and the writing is definitely instrumental, with both hands covering a lot of ground! Light arms and active fingerwork needed here.

The underlying harmonies follow traditional models and hopefully students will have already come across such IV-V-I cadential patterns before. If not, get them to practise them in different keys so that they see this six-note pattern as one unit, with an elegant phrasing away once the tonic is reached. There are few musical directions given by the composer, perhaps because it would have been played on a harpsichord, but we should add dynamic and articulation detail on the piano. Try using a contrasting dynamic for the varied repeats, although the editorial suggestion is equally valid. Get students to decide – that way they are more likely to remember to change the sound! Articulation needs to reflect the style of the minuet. So, for instance, slurring the quavers in bars 2 and 4 will help to emphasise the downbeat. The decorations add lightness and agility to the rather sturdy original, and students may like to add more détaché to these sections.

Reichardt   Allegretto   Trinity Guildhall

When an experienced pianist sees the first bar of this piece, they immediately recognise it as an A major broken chord and, having processed that, they barely read individual notes, instead noticing the general shape, rhythm and articulation. There is so much information to take in visually, yet aurally the effect is simple, direct and memorable. So, instead of getting students to read the opening, try first improvising around the broken chord, making sure the notes are secure, then playing it in a variety of patterns ending with the one here.

Reichardt was a prolific composer and Kapellmeister to both the flute-playing Frederick the Great and Frederick William II. The opening bar has the character of a fanfare, calling us to attention. It would be perfectly stylistic to double dot here, making the first semiquaver into a demi-semiquaver, but either will be acceptable for the exam. Note that in bar 4 the dotted quaver–semiquaver rhythm finishes the phrase so will need to be handled differently and played as written. Another ambiguous notation is found in bar 16: surely Reichardt didn't really want us to hold the bass minim after the upper parts had been released?

Most important is the work's character. *Allegretto* means 'fairly bright and lively' and keeping the rhythms precise will help this. Detached quavers will add lightness, along with careful interpretation of the slurs. The second note in a two-note slur is lighter and shorter, even when it occurs across the beat, as in bars 18 and 20. The snapped Scottish rhythms (bars 9, 10 etc.) need nifty fingerwork. There may be a temptation to put the longer note on the beat but a good way of avoiding this is to find a two-syllable word that stresses the first syllable (e.g., tiger rather than giraffe), and set this to the music.

Tchaikovsky   Old French Song   Trinity Guildhall

Young pianists are blessed by having many great composers who wrote specifically for children. Schumann and Prokofiev also come to mind, and this *Old French Song* is a gem from Tchaikovsky's collection (French was the language often spoken by the Russian aristocracy then). *Assai* means 'very', not to be confused with the French *assez*, which is 'quite', and students who can sustain the melody well may want to err on the slow side of the suggested metronome mark.

The notes should not take long to learn as the same melody is heard three times, but mood is all; without a strong sense of the emotional landscape behind this, a performance will sound bland. The actual sound chosen for the melody needs to be warm enough to sing above the lower parts, and aim for a flexibility in the pulse, aided by a relaxed suppleness in the hand itself. To help the part-playing in the left hand, suggest playing this with both hands, noticing the minim B♭ in bar 2, contrasted with the crotchet B♭ in bar 4. The *staccato* in the central section could be thought of as a cello *pizzicato* – the strings do ring for a moment after being plucked, so the notes need not be too short.

Some discreet pedalling could be helpful, although not essential. The addition of the alto line in the penultimate bar adds piquancy, but it is still the top line that needs to sing, so perhaps bring up the dynamic on the previous phrase, so that there is room for manoeuvre.

Khachaturian   A Little Song   Trinity Guildhall

There are so many repeated notes and chords in the accompaniment to this rich melody, that the pedal is really essential. *Legato* pedalling, with the foot moving up as the next chord is played, then down to sustain it before the hand releases. It may be easier to set up a pattern and change pedal on each chord, but ultimately it would be good for students to understand why the pedal could be held down for some bars, and need changing more often in others.

Khachaturian, with Shostakovich and Prokofiev, was publicly reprimanded by Stalin for his 'formalist trends and bourgeois ideology'. Nevertheless, he wrote operas, ballets, film scores and some enchanting music for children. Those falling semitones never fail to create a sad mood, and the key of C minor and Khachaturian's direct, expressive melody combine to tug at the heartstrings. Find a rich, singing sound for the melody, using plenty of arm-weight, and avoid becoming too soft in bar 9, to make a real effect with the sudden *p* in the following bar – a completely new colour or instrumentation. If pianists understand the semitone descent in the left-hand chords, they should be able to find them more easily and then can simply concentrate on the places where they deviate from this. Of course, the broken sixths in the second section are the thirds inverted.

Throughout there needs to be a good balance between the hands, putting the spotlight firmly on the melody. The mordents must be approached lyrically (rather than being 'bitten' as their name implies). The final phrase is heavy-hearted, the syncopations trying to pull the tempo back as the depressed tune plunges into left hand territory.

Swinstead   The Piebald Circus Pony   Trinity Guildhall

This could be one of those small, elegant ponies, trotting unhurriedly and somewhat aristocratically around the ring. Perhaps one of the dancers is performing acrobatic tricks on his back, which is why he needs to keep a calm, measured pace – 'without rubato' as Swinstead writes.

The musical detail helps to make the picture three-dimensional. Accents in bars 3 and 7, but not towards the end; *f* and *staccato* in bar 9, but *f* and accented in bar 13; *staccato* quavers in bars 8 and 20, *legato* elsewhere. The *mp* in bar 15 logically should begin on the second beat of that bar and note that although there is no *diminuendo* marked before the return of the opening music, a small one in the last two or three beats of bar 22 would be perfectly acceptable.

One of the most challenging aspects of this piece is precisely to keep it under control, not to let the tempo increase, not to allow the outer sections rise above a *p* dynamic. Then the *staccato* needs to be very neat and precise. A gentle wrist movement is needed, with added weight for the accents and perhaps a finger change for the Ds in the first bar – the small sideways movement helps to prevent tension in the hand. Remember too that dynamics are relative and finding the right character or mood is a better guide to sound. This may begin and end softly, but the pony is performing, its rider wears a sparkling costume, so the *p* here has a controlled energy and quiet confidence.

Ponce	Homage to Villanueva	Trinity Guildhall

Manuel Ponce was a Mexican composer who was interested in Mexican traditional songs. However, here he uses a mazurka, originally a Polish dance, to pay homage to Villanueva (new town). The harmonies Ponce chooses are fairly traditional, but the piece has an unusual flavour, with its short, lilting motifs and, before the pauses, the sort of flourishes that could easily come from a guitar.

Some pedalling could be of benefit, to sustain the harmonies, enriching the sound under the melody on its second and fourth appearances, and to link the repeated notes in the central section. Here the dotted line shows that the right hand melody descends to the top note of the left hand chord (in bars 22 and 24). It may be useful to practise the melody alone, making sure that the sound of that left hand note matches the right hand – not easy! In bar 27 playing the resolution, the B, with the right hand is recommended. There are other places – for instance the part-playing a few bars later – where re-arranging the hands could result in a better *legato*, or a more singing tone in the melody. Experiment!

A strong sense of nostalgia pervades the piece, suggested by the descending semitones in the bass, the falling sequences of the tune. Most phrases begin on the second beat, Ponce's nod to the mazurka style, but also a way of avoiding strong downbeats. Although a dance, there should be no rigidity in the pulse; the mood is thoughtful. Enjoy the moment of silence at the pauses, but *a tempo* for the ensuing cadences.

Hengeveld	Petite valse française	Trinity Guildhall

For those with a lyrical bent, the Grade 3 syllabus is a goldmine! The Dutch composer Hengeveld has written this tender French waltz with great affection, but to project this in performance needs sensitive listening and layering of lines.

Concentrate first on finding a round, supported sound for the bass notes, with a little extra weight on the dissonant F♯ to enable the *diminuendo* to make its mark. As far as possible, make a finger *legato* between these notes, then add in the chords, perhaps with the right hand at first, keeping them light and detached in the first two bars, with again a little extra sound in bar 3 so that the D♯ and A taper into the resolution on to D♮ and G♯. Once pianists are able to control and combine these two parts, they can then add a *cantabile* melody on top, feeling the weight of the arm behind supple fingers. This sort of writing is common and finding the right balance of sounds will be transferable to many other pieces. Worth spending time on.

The piece remains within a $\boldsymbol{p}$ framework, undisturbed by the small *crescendos*. Using pedal would be perfectly appropriate, but it works equally well without (although try to use it in the final bars). As with other lyrical dances, such as the previous piece, there is a gentle flexibility in the pulse. This can be felt in bar 2 and elsewhere, where the melody momentarily halts and the hand lifts, before finding the cadence, a combination of shaping the sound and of feeling the space, the uncertainty, in the quaver rest.

Garścia	Almond Tree	Trinity Guildhall

This enchanting piece by pedagogue Garścia has some elements in common with the previous French waltz. Here the slower pulse and the more static melody and harmony lead to a different treatment of the accompaniment. The bass notes still sustain and need a little more weight behind them than the syncopated chords. But syncopation can have two contrasting effects: it can lend excitement and forward movement, or a sense of heavy-heartedness, of pulling the pulse backwards. Here the general mood of the piece suggests the latter, so the chords, albeit lighter in touch than the bass or melody, will need to be held. The pedal will do this most effectively, but it is still good to feel the length of the chords, their unwillingness to be released, in the fingers. Too often the pedal is used as cover for poor *legato* – not something to encourage at this early stage!

There is an expressive *mf* at the opening, with a lightening of the arm and fingers for the fourth bar. Resist any temptation to hurry through the emptiness at the end of each bar. At first the words come slowly, then suddenly on the second line the floodgates open and the words pour out. This is wonderfully passionate writing, with the dissonance between the C♯ and C♮, the increased tempo and the gradual return to the opening sadness.

Sleight of hand is needed in bar 19; the left hand needs to release the B before the right hand needs it. The *meno mosso* will help. There are not so many notes to learn – lines are repeated – but the challenges are in interpretation and balancing sounds.

Milne	Grouch	Trinity Guildhall

The swung rhythm that Milne asks for is really only an approximation towards what 'real' jazz pianists play. They use articulation and stress, putting more weight on the second of two quavers, seeming to change the rhythm. For those trained more classically, playing duplet rhythms as triplets is the next best thing! The title is wonderfully evocative – no need to soften the sound politely as you release at the ends of phrases here. Instead the wedge implies a *staccato* with attitude! Let the arms swing a little as they swap quavers, especially in bars 3-4. Feel the drop-float (well, not so much of the float in this piece!) coming right from the back and shoulders for the grouchy *f*.

This will be an easy choice for many pianists. It is enormous fun to play, uncomplicated and with many repeats of ideas. Examiners will be well aware of this, so will expect a good tempo, observation of all the detail (dynamics in the repeated phrases, accents, *staccato* versus wedge etc.), and precise, firm fingers. Notice the length of the chords in the middle section; once or twice they release with the right hand, but more often they are sustained under the right hand's shorter note, or should come off in the middle of a right-hand lick (as in bars 10 and 14). The *sfz* towards the end needs extra energy in the fingers and thrust from the arm. The last two bars cover over five octaves in the right hand. Feet will need to be firmly placed and body weight well-balanced on the stool to enable this.

Kirnberger	Le Lutin (from *Piano All Sorts* Grades 2-3)	Trinity Faber

As previously noted, Johann Philipp Kirnberger was one of J S Bach's pupils and it is easy to trace the baroque master's influence here. The mischievous delight in springing around the keyboard suits the title of 'Little Imp', but the writing is strictly in two parts and the strong articulation suggests a dance. (There is surely a missing slur in the left hand in bar 3: it should be played as marked in bar 11.)

Semiquavers should be played *legato*; two-note slurs will need to use the 'drop-float' technique; crotchets should be played non-*legato* as Kirnberger, or the editor, requests and all other quavers will use a spritely *staccato*. Notice that the left hand takes over the theme in the fourth bar, and again when the opening returns towards the end. The accompanying right-hand semiquavers will need lots of careful repetition so that attention can be paid to characterising the theme in the bass. The hand needs to feel firm yet supple so that it can easily move around the keyboard while maintaining clear articulation.

This is energetic, colourful writing. Dynamic contrasts should be strongly projected and think of the *ritardando* at the end as being a broadening out, ending with a healthy *f* tone – this imp enjoys life!

| Schumann | Fröhlicher Landmann (The Merry Peasant) | |
| | (no. 10 from *Album for the Young* op. 68) | Wiener Urtext *or* Peters |

Schumann's *Album for the Young* began life as a few pieces written for his daughter's seventh birthday in 1848. He then expanded the collection, saying that he had never been in such a good mood as when he was composing these pieces. That good mood is definitely present in this famous teaching piece, although it is also quite a challenging choice.

'Fresh and cheerful' are Schumann's directions. It is all too easy to cloud the texture and the mood with over-heavy chords, so listen carefully for a good balance between the parts. The *f* dynamic really refers to the melody, whichever hand it is in; the accompanying chords can be kept at a discreet *mp* level. When the melody is played by both hands, either in octaves or in tenths, it may be easier for some students to divide the chords between the hands – for instance in the second half of bar 9 and the first half of bar 11. Note that in bars 1 and 2 the chords are detached quavers, but in bar 3 some chords are crotchets and should be held as such.

In keeping with its positive, outgoing mood, the general dynamic is *f*. However, within that, the phrases will need shaping, with Schumann's repeated *f* indications implying that the ends of previous phrases will probably have come down in dynamic. Choose a fairly steady tempo; unlike many of us nowadays, battling our way home through the rush hour, this peasant still seems full of energy after his day's work and is in no enormous hurry to get home.

| Heller | Étude in D (from *Piano All Sorts* Grades 2–3) | Trinity Faber |

Stephen Heller was born in Budapest, Hungary, but spent most of his life in Paris. He may not have the stature of his fellow pianist-composers Chopin and Liszt, but his short studies and pieces, many of which are teaching material, are usually full of character and inspire the imagination as well as train the fingers.

We talk about 'playing' the piano, but that element of play, of having fun, is too often missing. The *scherzando* character that Heller asks for in this study is not always easy to achieve but adding rhythmic poise, strong dynamic contrasts and a light *staccato* touch will greatly help. The groups of four semiquavers followed by either a *staccato* note or a minim need to be visualised as one gesture, one flexible movement, incorporating an accent on the first note. The *portamento* crotchets should be weighted, not too short. The sections in which one line is shared between the hands are probably the most difficult. Listen for perfectly even semiquavers and a seamless join between the hands – the exact division can be rearranged if necessary.

It should be easy to have fun with the middle section. Hold those minims – perhaps imagining an echo of the semiquavers in the rest and exaggerate the difference between the peremptory f demand and the nervous p response. Try to judge the length of the pause not by counting, but by sensing the dramatic tension set up in the preceding bars. Note that the tempo is only *moderato*; characterisation is what is important here, not speed.

Gurlitt	Impromptu op. 224 no. 5	
	(no. 16 from *Hours with the Masters* book 2)	Bosworth

To divide, or not to divide: that is the question. Whether 'tis nobler to play those initial semiquavers with the right hand, or to play safe and take the first two with the left … If you decide on the former, you may find that beginning 2 1 and then stretching up to the C may be a more secure fingering. The slur over these three bars is to show the phrasing; the chords in bar 2 should be played with a strong *staccato*, unlike those in the *con anima* section (note – this means with soul, not necessarily with a more animated tempo), which use a *mezzo staccato* touch, a sense of transferring the weight from one chord to the next. The *a tempo* in bar 33 implies that the preceding left-hand solo will have slightly slowed down.

Some of the suggested pedalling is there to enhance the tone quality rather than help with the *legato*. Listen to ensure that when such direct pedalling is used – when the pedal is marked to be depressed with a note or chord – it doesn't also catch the preceding notes. Not a problem if, as in bar 33, there is a rest before the pedalled chord, but in bar 31 the pedal should be depressed just *after* the D sounds, ensuring that the preceding Eb has been released. Other pedal markings are questionable: why not pedal the first pp chord in the beautiful chorale-like section? And why suddenly add pedal to the *staccato* chords in the fourth bar from the end? If you can answer these questions satisfactorily, then observe the directions. If not, alternatives are allowed!

This Impromptu lives up to its title, changing mood several times. Fortunately several of the phrases are repeated, so it will not take so long to learn. But once the notes are securely under the fingers, the challenge will be to find the right character and sound for each section.

Beach	Secrets op. 25 no. 5	
	(from *American Piano Repertoire* level 1)	Faber

Amy Beach was an American pianist and composer, writing, amongst other things, a piano concerto and many beautiful songs. There is considerable sophistication in this piece and, as pedalling is an essential ingredient, only those who can reach the pedal comfortably (heel kept on the ground) should choose it.

There are several methods of practising *Secrets*. Playing two chords per bar will make the harmony clear and therefore give clues to the phrasing. For instance, in bars 3 and 4, appoggiaturas within the first minim resolve during the second, implying a slight *diminuendo* through the bar. Each time the opening music returns it takes a different direction during the second phrase, and pianists need to be sensitive to this harmonic structure, so that the sound can reflect these shifting modulations. There are also melodic lines hidden within the texture, in the bass and the top parts. These should be isolated and practised with a good *cantabile* tone, so that when the other notes are added, they still sing in the foreground. The whole piece has a *dolce* atmosphere and even the *f* climax on the second page should not be too strident. Experiment with the pedalling here – the *legato* pedalling required elsewhere will need to be modified during these two bars of scalic figures, but do use some pedal, perhaps clearing it towards the end of each bar.

Poldini	The Enchanted Castle (from *Musical Moments Suite*)	Ricordi

This enchanted castle seems to be viewed from a distance, with partly held breath. The music suggests magic and wonderment, mist rising from the moat and shadows glimpsed dancing on the turrets! Although Ede Poldini has added many musical details, the general atmosphere is gentle, mysterious, understated. It needs a strong imagination and a sensitivity to harmonic colour to perform well.

Poldini is clearly concerned about the phrasing and he has marked *staccato*s where the hand should lift at the end of slurs. These *staccato*s should not be overdone – just a gentle release at the end of the bar, allowing a slight stress to fall on the beginning of the next phrase. Notice that the two 'slurs' in the left hand between bars 4 and 5 carry different instructions: the top one is a tie, whereas the lower one implies a *legato* between the two notes. There is an obvious misprint in bar 34: the last note in the right hand should be a quaver.

Dynamics are always relative and although the level rarely rises above *mf* here, it is important to leave room for the *pp* phrases to project. Rather than thinking of an absolute *p* or *pp*, it is usually more helpful to think of the mood and colour that need to be projected. Observe the rapid dynamic changes in the second section – not easy! Although the soundscape throughout is generally soft, it should also be warm and singing; let the fingertips stay alive to the feel of the keys depressing and keep the wrist and hand flexible – 'toujours la souplesse'!

Carroll	The Elfin Harp (from *Forest Fantasies*)	Forsyth

Walter Carroll wrote so much wonderful teaching material, but he is perhaps in need of a makeover. It is not just the titles that could be changed, but also the pedal markings: often his suggested pedal holds for an uncomfortably long time (look at bars 21-23 – doesn't your foot itch to change on the last beat of bar 23?) and in other places what he seems to be asking for is overly complicated. Pedalling exactly as marked in the first bars, i.e. direct pedalling on the first beat of the bars, lifting on the third, is actually more awkward than straightforward *legato* pedalling, beginning with the upbeat and changing on the first and third beats of the bar. Of course, Carroll is in good company; many other composers (or publishers) mark their pedalling in a similar manner, but the point is that the matter is open for debate and as long as pedalling is done correctly and used appropriately for this style, it will be acceptable.

A gentle movement of the hand, led from the wrist, will help the harp arpeggiations. At the beginning these chords are accompaniment, but towards the end they become more important and the top note must carry the melody. The broken chords that are shared between the hands must not audibly show where the hands change over: listen for a seamless *legato*, achieved again through flexibility in the hand and wrist. So much other musical detail to add – try playing it to students and ask them to spot where you leave out a dynamic change, a *rit*. or the *una corda*!

Teaching Notes 2009-2011

Mower	Fingersnap (from *22 Treats for Piano*)	Itchy Fingers

An unusual piece, Mike Mower asks for the quaver rhythms to be swung – apart from the last three in the left hand. The *tenuto* mark on the first right hand quaver is probably an attempt to reproduce the sense of accent on unstressed notes that in fact produces a genuine jazz swing. Some fingering has been given, but there are several places where a good fingering will still need to be found that suits the performer's hand. The middle section needs to move around the keyboard with ease and movements will need to be practised so that they are easy and smooth. Do not reject using a thumb on the black notes – a good idea in bar 14 for instance.

Students often find these jazzy rhythms quite easy. Watch out though for bar 10 where the second chord is not syncopated and perhaps get them to fill the rests in bars 17 and 18 with imaginary notes or words to make sure they are the right length.

Rozin	Woodpecker Waltz (from *Jewels & Gems*)	Fischer

Musically, this is very straightforward and should appeal to younger students, but there are also some useful aspects of technique to be practised here. Keep the right-hand repeated notes light, allowing the hand to change position as the fingers change and avoiding any sensation of tension or strenuousness. The tempo is only moderate. When the repeated notes occur *f* in the left hand, let the arm help to produce the initial accent.

This sort of accompaniment, with a sustained bass note and *staccato* chords, is very common. Check that students are not tensing their hands to hold down the bass note. The arm needs to stay flexible so that the *staccato* chords can be played very gently, not making the texture too thick. Aim for a fingering that enables a *legato* in the bass line, changing fingers if necessary, but check that there is no blurring between the bars when using the pedal as Albert Rozin directs.

The dynamics in the second section feel somewhat uncomfortable at first – for instance, a *diminuendo* in bar 20 would seem to make more sense than a sudden p – but stick with them and try to make them sound convincing! After all, there is something quite mechanical about the sound of a woodpecker pecking. Note the different markings for the right hand chords: accents, *staccato*, *tenuto* and, finally, *mezzo staccato*.

Intermediate level

At Intermediate level (Grades 4-5), candidates will typically be able to support their intentions in performance by demonstrating a sound understanding of material, leading to a more personal and imaginative interpretation, in which there is a reasonably consistent application of developing technical skills. Performances will be clear and well-projected with appropriate volume, control of pace (including variations in speed), control of tone quality and appropriate application of instrumental colour (e.g. vibrato, tone control) to support mood and character. Candidates will show evidence of sensitivity to and considerable control of material. Effective preparation and study will lead to a secure, accurate and sustained performance which will engage the audience. These features will be demonstrated through material which is substantial enough to convey some development, in terms of both the composer's intentions and the candidate's interpretation. Content will be sufficiently complex to provide some internal contrast and range (e.g. the preparation and achievement of climax, or a ternary form movement with a contrasting middle section). There will be a stylistic variety of musical language and form. Some subtleties of syntax will provide opportunity for a variety of approaches and interpretative choices (e.g. choice of articulation patterns in a movement from a Baroque suite).

Grade 4

Group A

Benda	Sonatina in A minor	Trinity Guildhall

Benda was born in Bohemia, ten years before Haydn. He was best known for his operettas, cantatas and melodramas, whilst two of his brothers became concertmasters for Frederick the Great.

This Sonatina looks quite black on the page, but many of the semiquavers fit into well-known scale or broken chord patterns. It could be useful to isolate these – for instance the opening arpeggio, divided between the hands, is played in A minor, E major, C major and G major. The falling sixths and thirds in the right hand could also be practised separately, and note that the third and fourth lines on page 2 are basically a sequence – that oft-used trick of stating something in the supertonic key, so that the sequence a tone lower will return us to the tonic.

Some of the virtuosity and drama of the piece comes from dividing one line of music between the two hands, confusing the listener into thinking one hand is managing all those notes. This happens in the opening, but also more awkwardly in the middle section, where the two hands rapidly replay the same note. Dexterity is needed here; remember that you do not even need to lift the finger off the key before repeating it, and staying close to the keys, just as in trills, will probably help. There should also be a tonal difference between the main melody note (left hand) and the accompaniment (right hand) – unlike the opening, where the rocket launch should be seamless between the two hands.

Ornamentation in this period is open to many interpretations and it could be argued that the mordent in bar 42, preceded by the upper note, should begin on the D♯. Ultimately this is less important than the musical effect, which should be one of tension on the E (as an appoggiatura) and release as it resolves on to the D♯. Keep the fingers nimble but light and without stiffness for the mordent.

Frey	Rondino	Trinity Guildhall

There is little information to be found about the German composer, pianist and teacher Martin Frey (1872-1946), but this Rondino seems to be written in a quasi-baroque manner and he may have composed it to help his own students assimilate the style. Compared to the colourful Saltarello or the circus atmosphere of the Trick Cyclist, this Rondino may not be as immediately attractive to some students, but much of the first page is repeated on the second and the suggested tempo is relatively sedate, so in terms of length and technical challenges this is not the most difficult choice.

The phrasing has been very precisely marked and, in most places, also dictates the articulation. The main difficulty of the piece is encountered immediately in bar 2: the right hand stresses the first quaver and lightly releases the second, whilst the left slurs three quavers, only releasing on the third. Hopefully this coordination problem will have been conquered elsewhere, but if not, it will need careful practice. It occurs throughout; note that in bars 5 and 6 the bass crotchets will be held longer than the released quavers in the treble, and the phrasing in the bass in bar 23 is unusual and somehow counter-intuitive – but consistently used, so clearly intentional.

Much of the writing is in two parts and, to add some variety of colour, you may get pianists to emphasise one hand in the first section and then another when the same music repeats – if they can achieve contrasting dynamics and articulation in each hand, they are doing really well! Both hands have small phrases that cover well over an octave. Ensure that the arm is aware of its role here to take the hand to the new position, and avoid lifting too far off the keyboard – a certain recipe for missing notes. The A minor section is an oasis of calm *legato* but disappointingly short.

Schmoll	Saltarello	Trinity Guildhall

At a good tempo this piece could sparkle, but the concomitant difficulties would then probably take it beyond Grade 4 level. So we are left with a rather sedate jumping dance, which needs careful attention to detail to make it musically viable.

The broken chord figuration in the left hand is common, but not always easy to control well. A good hand position is vital – the little finger must be supported and not allowed to collapse. A good exercise away from the piano to help strengthen the first knuckle joints is simply to put the hands flat on the legs, and then pull the fingertips in towards you, watching each one curve up into a claw position. If the little finger plays on its side (like a karate chop) the sound is bound to be uneven both rhythmically and tonally.

The *ff*s evoke the energy of a dance – spirited and fun, but not at all aggressive. This is particularly important towards the end, where the capricious changes from *ff* to *p* need to be carefully planned: too much weight on the *ff* will make the gear change into *p* almost impossible.

The D major section, with its cheeky D♯s, is delightful and flirtatious. Find a gentler colour here, well balanced but unobtrusive chords, and subtle phrasing that delivers the required *crescendos* and *diminuendos* without stepping outside the general quiet dynamic level. The metronome marks are a guide and you may like to try this a little faster. But beware – all that jumping around can make it easy to trip up …

Wilkinson	The Trick Cyclist	Trinity Guildhall

This piece falls into a similar category as the previous one. At the suggested speed it is manageable but feels too sedate for the circus acrobatics of a trick cyclist. So once students have successfully negotiated its obstacle course, you may like to push that upper metronome mark a little higher. By no means obligatory!

There are quite a few traps to look out for. See that *sfz* in bar 4? Notice that when Wilkinson brings back the opening, he deceptively places the *sfz* on the second beat and then follows it by a cheeky *p* in the treble. The right/left interweaving of chords in *f* are immediately followed by jumps to a change of position in both hands – and the composer annoyingly marks these *p* (bars 13-20). A sensitive control of arm-weight is needed here. Make sure students practise this quick change of direction.

The phrasing in the bass from bar 21 needs attention to bring out the smaller groups on the second page, but the *crescendo* from *mf* to *f* is extremely difficult over six bars and some discreet amendment may be necessary, for instance, coming down to *mp* as the *crescendo* begins. Note the different note lengths in each hand in the following bars, and you may like to try imagining the right hand moving into the keys, towards the lid, as it rapidly repeats the chords to help prevent tension.

J S Bach	Prelude in C minor, BWV 999 (from *Little Preludes and Fughettas*)	Any reliable edition

This little prelude is usually a firm favourite with young students. However, although the first bars are quickly learned, it is often difficult to maintain that speed of learning through the whole piece. Teachers will have different strategies for dealing with this, but perhaps give students an overview of the piece right from the beginning by playing it through with them and also by deciding on the shaping of the whole. Once they have a clear idea of the structure of the prelude, pianists will have a stronger sense of the final goal and be able to see how each new section they learn fits into this.

Maintaining a constant, almost hypnotic, pulse and understanding the harmonic structure are vital. The right hand should be practised as chords, with the first bass note of each bar, both to make the note-learning easier, but also so that choices can be made about phrasing and dynamics. The increasing left-hand intervals towards the middle of the prelude are usually accompanied by a gradual *crescendo*, but there are no hard and fast rules. There is definitely an increase in tension but this can be shown in different ways – of course, on the harpsichord, there was little possibility of such gradual dynamic progression.

The quavers in the left hand are normally detached and the last chord, with its *tierce de Picardie*, can be arpeggiated. In pieces such as these, Bach seems to look forward both to jazz and minimalism. A small masterpiece!

Handel	Entrée in G minor, HWV 453 no. 2	
	(no. 10 from *Handel Easy Piano Pieces and Dances*)	Bärenreiter

In the baroque period Entrée was usually the name given to an instrumental piece played before the ballet, but Handel may have been using the name here as an alternative to prelude or praeludium. Modifications can be made later if need be, but it would be sensible to make some decisions about articulation from the very beginning. The possibilities are numerous. Aim for consistency, using the same articulation for repeats of the same figure.

Handel was remarkably prolific, even if he did at times resort to reusing his own, or others', music. This movement reflects that; the music seldom repeats, but seems to progress quite organically in a continuous stream. This of course poses its own problems for performers. Find repeated patterns and figures to make the initial learning process simpler. For instance, the cadential figure in bar 12 returns in the tonic in bars 17 and 19.

The left hand should not be a passenger in this music. Not only does it have the main voice in places, but its role as director of the harmonic progressions is important. It often makes the phrasing clear. Although the first phrase begins with a quaver upbeat, the bass line makes it clear that the next phrase begins after the cadence on the crotchet upbeat. The next perfect cadence, in the relative major, occurs in the middle of bar 5, making the phrase lengths unusually complex.

The addition of dynamics is left up to the performer. They need to reflect the shape and pitch of the melodic line as well as the harmonic structure. The trill in bar 6 must begin on the upper note and notice that the last note of that bar is an F♮. Ultimately this Entrée needs to flow quite naturally and easily, with elegance and little sense of effort.

Haydn	Menuet & Trio from Sonata in D, Hob. XVI/4	
	(no. 9 from *Nine Little Early Sonatas*)	Henle

This Menuet and Trio comes from one of Haydn's early keyboard sonatas, written during his time with the Esterházys and probably intended as teaching material. It will be a sophisticated choice: there is more variety of texture and more demands made on the performer than in any of the other minuets looked at so far, and there is also the problem of the ornaments to address.

There are few hard and fast rules about ornamentation; choices need to be made between possible alternatives based on context. Generally the trills here will begin on the upper note, but not if the preceding note is the upper note (as in bar 21 for instance). There are two minim trills that have the upper note marked as an appoggiatura. One good solution here would be to make the appoggiatura into a crotchet, trilling on the second crotchet only. In later works Haydn often marked quite clearly when he wished a trill to end with a turn (or 'suffix'). Here it would be possible to add a turn if the note after the trill ascends, as in the penultimate bars of each part of the Trio. The appoggiatura in bar 8 can be played either as a crotchet or minim. Finally, it will be better at this stage (both for the style of the music and for young pianists) to make the ornaments quite measured, never allowing them to disturb the rhythmic flow.

Such an early-classical work as this sonata would still have been played on the harpsichord or clavichord and the bareness of the score reflects this. Performers are free to add their own articulation and dynamics, always keeping in mind the dance style. As in Beethoven's *German Dance* for this grade (see below), the Trio remains in the same key as the Menuet; contrast needs to be found by other means. Haydn's Trio, again like Beethoven's, is more lyrical; there is more constant quaver movement and the articulation will be smoother, accompanied by a gentler dynamic range.

| Beethoven | German Dance in B♭, WoO 8 no. 4 | |
| | (from *Ecossaises and German Dances*) | Peters |

There is a welcome ruggedness in many of Beethoven's German Dances, and this one, with its predominantly bright, primary harmonies, is no exception. One in the same key of B♭ was in the previous Grade 3 syllabus, and so this may be a good choice for someone who played that. There are plenty of new elements here, including right-hand octaves (non-*legato*) in the Trio, and it is another strong, enjoyable dance.

The speed need not be too fast; there is a more rugged energy to this dance than in the more aristocratic minuets. There is still a stress on the first beat of the bar, emphasised by Beethoven with two-note slurs or *sforzandos*. The Trio stays mostly in the tonic key, but is slightly more lyrical and generally softer. The *sforzandos* need to be modified here, a gentler accent within $\boldsymbol{p}$ pointing up the syncopation, rather than the $\boldsymbol{f}$ stresses on the appoggiaturas in the first section.

Use strong fingers for the accented acciaccaturas in the Trio, perhaps 35 rather than 45. Listen for balance between the hands, likely to be most problematic in the Trio when the left hand has its Alberti bass figuration. Throughout, many of the chords are in close position, so check that they do not become too thick and stodgy – the *German Dances* may be earthier than many, but they are still dances.

| Heller | Jägerbursch (The Huntsman), no. 4 from *5 Lieder ohne Worte* | |
| | (from *Music Book for Small Folks and Grown-ups* op. 138, book 1) | Universal |

This young hunting boy is full of energy as he rides his horse through the fields, before gradually disappearing out of sight. A bright tone colour is needed for this piece, strong fingerwork, plenty of help from the arm on the accents, and a crisp *staccato*.

Keep the elbows free as the arms move laterally to accommodate the broken chords. Also check that once the left hand has played the dotted crotchet chords that it returns to 'neutral', not keeping more pressure on the notes than is necessary. The accents add point and energy to the longer notes, but the sound must not get too heavy and thick, particularly when the pedal is held through bars. The opening figures also sound good if pedalled (bar 1, then *senza ped.* for bar 2 etc.) and this would allow pianists to play the dotted crotchets with an upward action of the wrist and an immediate release of the note, thereby producing the accent and a buoyant sound as well as preventing any tension.

The acciaccaturas in the middle will really muddy the texture if pedalled as marked. Changing the pedal on the half bar here, ensuring that the D♯ is not caught in the E^7 harmony is a suggestion. Very little, if any, *rubato* is needed in such a piece. Keep the pulse constant (the recommended metronome mark is excellent), particularly through the *diminuendo* at the end. The hunter disappears out of view, but does not slacken his pace.

Hounsome	The Optimist (from *Upbeat for Piano* level 3)	Subject

The rhythms and style of *The Optimist* should be easily captured by most students with a penchant for jazzy pieces. It will be easy to break up into small, learnable sections, with an introduction and theme in D, both of which return in C after a central section based in B♭. An unusual key structure!

The pulse maintained in the left hand needs to be strong, so that the many syncopations in the top part make their effect. Separate the crotchets without making them too *staccato*. Acciaccaturas seem to be reproducing the swoop up to the note favoured by many jazz singers and saxophonists, so can afford to be a little more melodic here. The long slurs indicate the phrasing, not necessarily implying that all underneath them needs to be played *legato*. Quite often notes or chords are repeated and so will need to be detached. To use too much pedal here would not be stylistic.

The exception is in the 'honky-tonk' section, where the pedalling will help these few bars sound enormously effective, with little effort! The right forearm needs to use a slight rotary motion to achieve the *tremolo* effect and the left hand will *crescendo* and *diminuendo* during each two-bar phrase. The whole piece should sound confident and upbeat, only relaxing the mood at the very end.

Group B

Purcell	Hornpipe	Trinity Guildhall

Henry Purcell was the greatest English composer of his time and revelled in such appointments as Keeper of the King's Keyboard and Wind Instruments and Composer for the King's Violins. He also became organist at Westminster Abbey and the Chapel Royal and whilst many works reflect the patronage of the monarch and the church, there are also many that are a result of his connection to the theatre.

This dance comes from Purcell's incidental music to *Abdelazar*, or *The Moor's Revenge*, and was immortalised by Benjamin Britten in his *Young Person's Guide to the Orchestra*, a set of variations on Purcell's melody to accompany a Ministry of Education film on the various instruments in the orchestra. Originally a hornpipe was a wooden piped instrument with a reed one end and a horn-like bell the other. It was often used to accompany dances, particularly those that were associated with sailors; hence the dance came to be known as a hornpipe.

The dynamics are editorial and reflect the idea of a full orchestra for the main theme, with instrumental solos playing the two intervening sections. This is highly logical, but not the only solution. Each statement of the theme could take a step up in terms of volume, or you could take a *f, p, f* approach. At the suggested tempo the theme has nobility and grandeur, and using blocks of dynamic may help to emphasise this, as well as being more stylistically appropriate. Similarly there are various articulation possibilities to be explored – encourage students to experiment! The exercises for this grade help with the playing of ornaments. So often we tighten the hand before them, worried about fitting all those notes in. Instead it is vital to keep the fingers firm but flexible, the wrist supple, and not to lift the fingers too high. Practise the trill slowly at first, keeping this in mind, before playing at tempo.

Kullak	The Ghost in the Chimney	Trinity Guildhall

Here we have Gothic melodrama! *Mit Verschiebung* towards the end literally means 'with displacement' or 'with shifting' and is a direction to use the *una corda* (in a grand piano, it displaces all the hammers to one side). The middle section also sounds better with some pedal, so long legs are needed.

This piece will only make sense if all the musical detail is interpreted and almost needs acting as much as playing. As well as following all the directions, try fitting a story to the music to really bring it alive. For example: there's a room that you are really scared to enter because you know a ghost lives there. You try once, but chicken out and play in the kitchen instead (the C major section). Then you are drawn back to the haunted room. This time you go inside, holding your breath ... BANG – a sudden noise and you run away, as the ghost quietly disappears once more up the chimney ...

Make sure that you have $^6_8$ firmly in your head before you start; it is tempting to play the opening semiquavers as triplets, with the accent on the top note. Notice all the rests, initially in the right hand only, but then in both. The quavers in bar 7 can also be quite short, and all this air in the sound can help to project a sense of fear. There is some tricky part playing in places and some redistribution of the hands (bars 14 and 46) may make this easier. Using pedal in the C major section is not obligatory, but it will immediately change the texture and mood, as well as avoiding bumpy repeated notes. Beware of the different left hand in bar 25 and be sure to make the most of the two pauses.

Prokofiev	Promenade	Trinity Guildhall

This is one of the gems of this grade and if you are not familiar with Prokofiev's other children's pieces it is worth looking out for them, published as op. 65, *Musique d'enfants*. The language is unmistakably his, the characterisation is strong and the pedagogy behind the pieces is sound.

The main theme seems nonchalant, but needs a good, singing *legato* touch. Feel the weight transferring from finger to finger, keeping the wrist supple and being particularly careful about judging the weight needed on the thumb. Meanwhile the left hand has a mix of *legato* triplets, with a gentle *staccato* release on the ensuing crotchet (keep the little finger supported here) and longer, but separated crotchets elsewhere – 'with a light touch' Prokofiev writes. Not easy to achieve and you may want to spend some time working hands separately.

The middle section also has its own challenges of part-playing and contrasted dynamics – this is where you meet and greet friends and acquaintances during your walk. Encourage students initially to play the two lines in the treble with two hands, so that they get used to hearing how one line fades as another enters. Tapping the pulse with a foot can prepare for the addition of the separated bass chords. In bar 43 (left hand) other editions have **_p_** marked on the second crotchet, as in bar 39, which seems logical. The *tenuto* marks from bars 45–49 could be interpreted as slight stresses to bring out the gradual return to C major in the right-hand chords.

The title suggests a Sunday afternoon, an unhurried walk in the fresh air and sunshine. The tempo is steady, but without rigidity. A slight slowing up in the last bar, for instance, would seem totally natural.

Cornick	Ragtime Blues	Trinity Guildhall

There seems to be an honourable custom of including a blues amongst the Grade 4 choices; the last two were by Edward Putz and both became firm favourites. Here the popular composer Mike Cornick takes on the mantle and merges blues with ragtime to create a fairly straightforward choice.

Blues grew from an oral tradition and have a specified harmonic structure: 12-bar patterns, divided into three four-bar phrases, coloured largely by chords of the tonic and subdominant. Normally there is a melodic line over the top, often improvised, and the mood is bittersweet. Ragtime is far more upbeat, dominated by syncopations and the sort of energy that made it into a popular dance. Scott Joplin is the most celebrated composer of ragtime and, despite the syncopation, the tempi are often fairly relaxed. Cornick has made a synthesis of these two styles, although it seems that the ragtime element is stronger, with an absence of real melodic content and a 16-bar structure.

A rounded hand shape will be best for balancing the chords successfully; aim to focus attention on to the top notes in the right hand to prevent the chords from sounding anonymous. In ragtime the quavers are played as written, *not* swung. The same music is basically repeated twice, with a small prelude and postlude, and examiners – well aware that this is a relatively easy choice – will be listening out for all the detail of dynamic and articulation to be very precise.

Rodney Bennett	Saturday's Child	Trinity Guildhall

'Saturday's child works hard for a living' according to the nursery rhyme, and Bennett has written a piece with strong accents and plenty of energy to depict this. British composer Richard Rodney Bennett has an eclectic style, equally at home playing jazz as in writing film scores (*Four Weddings and a Funeral* being the most celebrated!) but here the style is modern and edgy. At the right tempo, this is also the shortest choice for Grade 4.

There are two places where Bennett calls for *ff* and accents. Play these chords right from the back with firm fingertips, but without tensing the arms. They can then be used as a guide for the other dynamic levels: *f* and *mf* with accents must be one or two steps down in dynamic to prevent the whole piece from shouting. Notice that in the main musical idea, the accents occur only every fourth bar, making the phrase shape clear. The 3, 3, 4, 3 content of each 4-bar phrase is maintained until bars 24-32, where the accents (rather than the barlines) ask for a 6, 2 effect over each two bars. It may be useful to get pianists to feel comfortable with these rhythmic patterns away from the piano, using words or movement.

Bennett has asked for a slur between the upbeat and the first chord at the beginning and elsewhere. This is difficult as the upbeat note is immediately repeated by the left hand, so needs to be released by the right hand. It is possible to use the pedal to connect the notes, but this is asking for very quick and demanding coordination at Grade 4 level. If students can reach the pedal easily, they may like to try it – it is simple to do at the very beginning. But if the right hand thumb holds the D for as long as possible, refusing to play it *staccato*, it will be perfectly acceptable and, in a good, high-octane performance, the non-*legato* will be barely noticeable.

| Haas | Hausmarch op. 53 no. 4 (no. 2 of Zwei Hausmärchen from *New Recital Book for Piano* vol. II) | Schott |

Hausmärchen are folk tales (literally house fairy tales) and this rather quirky piece needs a good sense of narrative. Dynamics are an important constituent: they vary widely and, at times, quite suddenly and mischievously. It is puzzling that the *f* in bar 5 is not replicated in bar 17 ... a misprint or an intentional change? Either choice should be acceptable. The top D just before the *pp* bars can easily be taken by the left hand.

Acciaccaturas are also an important element here. The one that occurs in the very first bar should be quite quickly crushed before the beat, ensuring that it is not caught in the pedal. However, those in the *pp* bars have more melodic and harmonic interest and also need greater tonal control – a different approach is needed there and these acciaccaturas sound good if they are caught in the pedal! These are a tricky four bars; be sure to identify the falling melodic line in the soprano. The pedal marks are somewhat ambiguous, as they are not always aligned with the third beat. The lively character of this folk tale would suggest that the third beat of such bars should be heard as a *staccato* and releasing the pedal on this beat will achieve that.

The music needs to dance, with crisp, light *staccato*s, and generally a small stress on the first beat of the bar. Have fun with the middle section. The sudden change of key to A♭ is quite preposterous and the link back to the opening is full of humour – strong dynamics will help. The B♮ in bar 51 sounds strange at first, but the music is about to change direction so that it ends in the tonic (rather than the dominant as was the case in its previous statements), and the B prepares the way for this change.

| Farr | For Salesi (from *Firestarters 1 – 14 Piano Miniatures*) | Promethean |

A gently romantic piece that needs sensitive control of sound and phrasing and good pedalling. Gareth Farr has indicated *rits* and *ralls*, but a sense of subtle *rubato* permeates this style; ultimately we should be aware of long lines of melody, not beats.

The entire piece remains within a *p* to *pp* framework and, with the accompaniment sometimes invading the general territory of the melody, the two lines will need to be carefully balanced. A relaxed lateral movement in the left forearm will help, and avoid any unintentional accents on the thumb. The melody should sing – the sound should always be supported by the arm and shoulder so that it projects and can be shaped. Ask students to sing the phrases, noticing how they can sustain the tone through the dotted crotchets. Hearing it like this will make them more aware of what they need to do to recreate that sense of *legato* on the piano.

It would be a good idea to play through the melody with the bass line alone to concentrate on the harmonies Farr has chosen. In places these are unexpected and quite beautiful; an awareness of them will help the ear direct the fingers to colour them so that the audience also notices them. The final section, where the opening music returns, needs to be played with great delicacy. The hands are now much further apart, lending more transparency to the sound, and the right hand plays in chords. Check that the melody is still the main line, shadowed by the lowest notes in the bass – the effect should be quite magical.

Miller-Stott	For Kate Edger, no. 2 of Votes for Women (from *First Fifteen –*	
	A Selection of Piano Music by New Zealand Composers)	SOUNZ

Kate Edger was born in England but moved to New Zealand when she was five and spent the rest of her life there. When she applied for a university scholarship (in the 1870s), she kept her gender a secret, was offered a place and thereby became the first woman in the British Empire to earn a BA. During the rest of her life she taught and worked for women's suffrage, helping to found the Society for the Protection of Women and Children.

Perhaps Ms Edger was also a jazz aficionado – otherwise there seems to be little connection between her history and this piece! Taken at a 'fast and jaunty' pace, the music sounds busy and somewhat eccentric. Rosemary Miller-Stott plays with the accents within the $\frac{6}{8}$ time signature, often flirting with $\frac{3}{4}$, sometimes in both hands, sometimes only in one. Conquering these cross-rhythms and sorting out all the articulation will be the challenges of this piece. It is often helpful to practise cross-rhythms separately from the printed notes, either just tapping on the piano lid or by using simple triads that will require little concentration on the notes themselves.

There is also a lot of humour here. Enjoy the sudden changes of direction, as in bar 13, the 'wrong' notes and the nonchalant ending – no *rallentando* is needed, but the penultimate chord is shared between the hands. Much of this needs a light touch: precision without exaggeration.

Grade 5

Group A

Couperin	Les Chérubins	Trinity Guildhall

Of the many musical Couperins, François – son of teacher Charles, and nephew of fellow-composer Louis – was the one nicknamed 'Le Grand'. Besides his compositions, he also wrote *L'Art de Toucher le Clavecin* ('The Art of Playing the Harpsichord'), a masterly treatise on fingering, touch and ornaments which much influenced J S Bach. His four volumes of keyboard music contain more than 230 pieces, collected into 27 'Ordres' or suites; the fourth book (containing the 20th 'Ordre', from which *Les Chérubins* comes) dates from 1730.

Recreate the mood of the time (gracious and tasteful) with a non-pedalled style and the clear dynamic contrasts characteristic of the harpsichord. Articulation should be particularly neat for the ornaments: notice that the one in footnote (1) stops just before the low F bass note. Try all the printed fingerings, but if bars 34-35 seem awkward try right hand 1352 1351/2353 1352 instead. Typically for the time, dynamics are not printed, but left to the interpreter. Clues – not just in this piece, but in Baroque music as a whole – exist within the music itself. Exactly repeated phrases (at the same pitch) may be treated as *p* echoes, for example, bar 12 beat 2 (echoing bar 4 beat 2), or the 'petite reprise' (from halfway through bar 20). When repeating this (as the footnote advises), go straight from bar 24 back to beat 2 of bar 20, without a break.

A change of texture may invite a change of dynamic: drop to *p* halfway through bar 28, for instance, if you were *f* before. High-pitched left hand, and/or a switch to the minor mode (as from halfway through bar 42), may suggest *p*. Try matching the same dynamics to recurring passages so as to clarify the structure: be *f* from halfway through bar 52, for instance, if you were *f* halfway through bar 24 (optionally dropping to *p* in the second beat of bar 54 if that's what you did in the second half of bar 26). Starting and finishing *f* is safe (though not compulsory) – and highly likely from bar 60, as the octaves in the footnote suggest. These could not fail to sound loud on the harpsichord: notice they are now all crotchets, unlike the otherwise similar bars 34-35 and 56-57. Dropping to *p* as early as bar 2 beat 2 may provide contrast, but you may prefer to sustain *f* until the piece has got further under way.

J S Bach	Menuet & Trio (from French Suite no. 3, BWV 814)	Trinity Guildhall

The French Suites were meant to be easier than the English ones, but bars like 8, 17-19 and 22 of this minuet and trio still need good co-ordination – these passages, plus the awareness that the minuet was a stately dance rather than a knees-up, suggest keeping a steady pace throughout. Studying other editions may be disconcerting. Some of them start with first two bass notes the other way round (to match bars 5 and 9). More drastically, other editions print Bach's original Menuet ending (bars 25-32), which, while preserving the same harmony, had many completely different notes. The album here chooses his revised version.

As with Couperin (see above), dynamics are left to the player. Section 1 ends in bright D major, so its closing phrase could be *f* and busy-textured bars 17-22 could stay *f*. Minor-inflected bars 25-26 could drop to *p*, with the higher-pitched sequence immediately following (bars 27-28) a little louder, and the ornate right hand with high notes from bar 29 could reach *f*. The Trio (called 'Menuet II' in some editions) is thoughtful and richly harmonised: it may possibly go a little slower and start softly. Check the ornament footnote (1), which shows that in performance treble C is pushed off the beat (bass D♯ synchronises with treble F♯ and A). High notes and a startling dissonance in bars 45-46 invite *f* treatment: bar 50's bright D major and detached high notes suggest that this could stay *f* until bar 53, which, if dropping to *p* and staying so until the end, will produce a pleasing arch-shape in dynamics and prepare for a contrasted *f* return to the minuet.

Dussek	Sonatina in G, op. 20 no. 1, 1st movement: Allegro non tanto	Trinity Guildhall

Jan Ladislav Dussek's music was immensely popular in his own lifetime, some of his pieces being reprinted up to ten times. Many reprints appeared under changed opus numbers, making correct identification something of a nightmare: this op. 20 piece also appeared as op. 19. Mozart had his Köchel: Dussek's cataloguer was named Craw, and this particular sonata is Craw no. 88.

Whatever its number, this Sonatina movement fills a whole sonata form in minimum time. The vigorous (fanfare-like) first theme and contrasting second (high register, and lyrical) are contained in just eight bars of exposition, modulating to the dominant (bar 8) then repeated in full (bars 9-16). The development (bars 17-24) actually uses new material; the recapitulation (bar 25) is marked *f* (rather than *mf*) in some editions, presumably to match bar 1 more exactly. Playing *mf*, however, shows the music in a fresh light – a bonus in such a short piece. The second theme starts roughly inverted on recapitulation (bar 29), and Dussek even makes room for a *Coda* (bar 34 onwards), imitating high trumpets in bar 35 and answering horns in bar 37. End strongly with a slight *rit.* (but no *dim.*) in bars 38-39. As always in this early-classical style, check note lengths before rests in the less busy hand (just a crotchet in the left hand of bars 8 and 17-20; *staccato* quavers in 21-24); be smooth in slurred two-part passages (right hand bars 1-3) and of course shade-off the very last cadence. Memorisers beware: bar 2's bass octave (with sustained lower note) does not recur in the otherwise identical bar 26.

Dussek's music, even though remarkably prefiguring Schubert, Mendelssohn and others, fell out of favour after his death, being displaced by the greater achievements of those later composers. One influence remains to this day, however: the practice of placing the piano sideways-on to the audience. This had not always been so: Dussek started it, mainly to show off his handsome profile, and of course it is the perfect position for the raised piano lid to reflect the sound into the concert hall.

McClure	Camel Ride	Trinity Guildhall

You've seen it in a thousand films: the slow, stately and dignified procession of a camel train across the desert. The reality is different: camels are truculent beasts and are ridden only under protest. The seated position is grossly uncomfortable, and you travel in a series of lurches, each one threatening to unseat you if not throw you to the ground. All this may be imagined in Paul McClure's delightful piece: the left hand provides the footprints, while the right hand depicts either the wailing music of the Middle East or else the unfortunate rider slithering around on the camel's back! The *meno mosso* is either a crossing over even unsteadier ground or – conversely – a point of comparative comfort, both pictures rudely awakened by the animal braying (repeated notes in bars 26-30) and digging in its heels (bars 31-32) as the rider whips the animal (repeated chords) in an effort to get it going. The journey resumes (bar 35), the rider sliding about even more unsteadily than before (right-hand grace notes, on or before the beat, as you prefer) and – matching the film image at last – fades into the distance before a final snort from the animal.

Spread the left-hand thumb across two notes in many places (e.g. bars 20-30 and, as marked, 32-34), aiming exactly between the two notes each time for safety. Check unexpected pitches: the second offbeat footprint uses different notes from the first (those notes a second apart); the top voice is not tied over barline 20/21 but moves to a different note; G♭ persists through bar 23 and E♭ through the left hand (but not the right hand) of bar 34. Check accidentals: bar 41's right-hand slither rises before it falls. The pace should halve at bar 18 and again at 52: the final bar's overall rhythm is quaver rest, two semiquavers, quaver with grace note. The very last C of all, marked to be played with the left hand, may be thumped instead with the right hand for extra force if it can be reached in time.

Couperin	Allemande in D minor (from *Baroque Real Repertoire*)	Trinity Faber

Like much French Baroque music this Allemande bristles with potentially fussy ornaments – but many of them are optional (see footnote in the score). In a concert performance the must-do ornaments could be played first time round, and the optional ones added on the repeats: otherwise mark with a pencil the ones you intend to play, and cross out the others (useful in bar 6, for instance). Prepare to score-read bars 11-12, synchronising the outer staves (with ornaments helpfully written out in full) and ignoring the middle one. With or without ornament, try re-fingering bar 1 with 23(23) 4 5323 1543; the finger-switching during bar 2's ornament however is a good idea, as are similar suggestions later.

The melody has some natural breaks – but add more, say between paired right-hand quavers in bars

5, 9 and 10. Couperin left no dynamics, so deduce your own from the texture. As a suggestion, start confidently at *mf*, drop to *p* after bar 3's cadence, and *cresc.* through bar 6 to *mf* at 7. High pitch in both hands (and bright key) after the repeat mark implies *f*; *dim.* to *mf* halfway through bar 9; 10 may start *mp*, *p* two beats later; *cresc.* to *mf* at 12 and *f* at 13. Stay firm, and broaden to the end with *pesante* semiquavers.

Beethoven	Bagatelle in D, op. 119 no. 3 [with repeats]	
	(from *Complete Bagatelles*)	Henle *or* Wiener Urtext

Check the bar-count: if you have four repeated sections and a total of 56 bars, then the bar numbers match ours – and in performance you play bars 1-32 (with all repeats), then 1-16 again (without repeats) then 33-56, with no break between sections. If the bar-count is different, then some repeats (and/or the *da capo* and *Coda* instruction) will have been written out.

Marked *à l'Allemande*, (♩ = maximum 72), this is nothing to do with the well-behaved slow $\frac{4}{4}$ allemandes of Bach's time, but gentle Bavarian thigh-slapping (that may remind you of the op. 28 Sonata's Finale) – and, from bars 17 and 33, less gentle clinking of huge beer glasses.
By op. 119 Beethoven's piano had extended its range well beyond the three-and-a-half leger line F he'd known earlier, and his opening ripple up to top D takes full advantage. Four-bar phrases persist throughout, even in the 'stuck in a groove' *Coda* where (as in bars 17-22) you can imagine the left-hand semiquavers boosted by a driving jazz bass on every quaver. Slur *cantabile* phrases in bars like 2/3-4, but underline rests after glass-clinking chords with crotchet pedals: some editions have full octave chords in bars 18, 34, 36 and 38 but others leave out the bottom note. Bar 23's trill is fast and strong; bars 24/25 and 53 are *f sempre*: the final pay-off is cheekily *p subito*, the opening ripple now ending (not starting) a four-bar phrase and closing not with the usual quaver but a held crotchet.

Kuhlau	Sonatina op. 55 no. 1, 3rd movement: Vivace	
	(from *Sonatinas* op. 20 & op. 55)	Kjos

German-born Friedrich Kuhlau (1786-1732) worked mostly in Denmark, and wrote extensively for the flute – maybe a hint to keep this well-known sonatina movement light and graceful. Count one-in-a-bar rather than three (say ♩. = 54-63), keeping the second quavers of bars 1-2 and 9-10 lighter than the downbeats for a bouncy rather than plodding effect. Control the right-hand fourth-finger crossover (barline 5/6) and potentially weak fingers in bar 7 to ensure evenness in semiquavers; similarly, avoid bumping the thumb in chromatic scales (bars 25-32, where the left hand also has a good tune, not just isolated chords). Try whole-bar pedals in bars 53-59 and 61-67 for contrast of tone and a warm sound. The *sf*s in bars 22 and 90 (and particularly 18 and 86, after *p* markings) are really only accents in the prevailing dynamic but the triplets in bars 112-113 may be *f subito*, and dramatic. *Rall.* slightly in bar 115 for a controlled finish.

| Kullak | The Race op. 81 no. 6 (from *Scenes from Childhood*) | Schirmer |

Theodor Kullak (1818-1882) is best known for his didactic *Octave School* (not surprising, perhaps, from a student of Czerny). The high point of his career was probably 1846, when he became court pianist to the King of Prussia. *The Race* needs good counting, to cope with military-style dotted (and double dotted) rhythms – and good scales a tenth apart (not an octave, notice). These – in fact, the whole piece – should sound quite well with no pedal at all, apart from the very last two chords, which may be pedalled for added richness.

Take the tempo (♩ = 112-132) not just from scales but also the left-hand fanfares of bars 10 and 18: these must be as clear as a drum. Count a whole bar in, to ensure a full crotchet *f* upbeat (bar 8 should probably match it; the printed dynamic may be misplaced). Practice bar 9 with accented Eb, A♮ and D to avoid running away, and with practice-pause on bar 23's quavers (and 24's downbeat) to get your bearings. Compare bar 12's left hand with 14's, similarly bars 20 and 22. Bar 26's *p* is on the second quaver, not the first; for refinements, *cresc.* into bar 4 to underline the modulation, *più cresc.* in 22 to emphasise the top note (higher than in 20), and be fleetingly sentimental in the *legatissimo* bar 17.

| Tchaikovsky | Song of the Lark (from *Romantic Real Repertoire*) | Trinity Faber |

This dates from 1878 – might Debussy have known it when composing his very similar Second Arabesque (1891)? The birdsong here needs a well-articulated right hand with controlled grace notes, confident sight reading among high leger lines, and sensitive left-hand chords to balance the right hand when in (weak) very high register. The suggested fingerings, changing on same-pitch notes, are designed for best articulation and phrasing: alternatively try starting bar 1 with 343, and bar 9 with 232 1 45. Lift left-hand fingers with care to avoid smearing B with C in bars 1-2; thereafter compare the lifted left-hand chords in bars 2/3, 6/7-8 and 12 with held (though preferably unpedalled) crotchets through bars 11 and 15-19. *Crescendo*s in bars 4 and 12 may reach more than *p*, the printed *p*s then being *subito*. Check for the correct right-hand octave in bars 12 and 16, memorise final bars 31-32 (to enable the student to see where their hands land) – and compare this little bird with Grieg's more serious one (op. 43 no. 4).

| Hedges | Vivace (no. 5 from *5 Concert Pieces for Young Pianists*) | Universal |

Antony Hedges' piece is lively and humorous, especially if you like odd rhythms but find Bartók too serious. The $\frac{7}{8}$ time signature here switches between 2+2+3 and 3+2+2; make the pattern changes easy to hear by marking the first notes of each group, usually with a strong driving left hand (e.g. the F♯ and Eb in bar 4, the three crotchets in bar 5, the G, A and F in bar 8). Hedges wittily wrong-foots his listeners (hopefully not the players) with the occasional dropped or extra beat (bars in $\frac{6}{8}$ or $\frac{4}{4}$ time).

For an energetic start without rushing, slightly separate the left-hand crotchets and finger the right hand either with 12 5 25 15 4 23/14 5 1 or else with thumb on every alto note. The more lyrical bar 9 (likewise 15 and 27) starts with right-hand 2, bar 10 (and 16) with 4; start bars 17 and 29 with 1, each slur of bar 11 likewise and those in bars 12-13 and 32-33 with 4. End bar 17 with 52 and bar 21 with 245 to best approach punchy chords in 22; bars 34/35 go 421 12 3412/13 5. Enjoy bar 38's slimy bass-line, cover bars 39–40's possibly unstretchable slurred tenths with quick pedals, and count (don't *rit*.) from bar 41 to the end, holding bar 43 with the pedal in order to prepare bottom-octave bar 44 against very fast grace notes.

Group B

Cimarosa	Sonata C. 49 (F. 49)	Trinity Guildhall

Don't turn the page hurriedly in the search for an easier piece: this dauntingly black-looking composition actually goes very slowly, and is perfect for expressive playing provided you can keep the endlessly repeating rhythm interesting. Take the tempo from footnote 2, whose demisemiquavers should be slow enough to sing: count a steady eight-in-a-bar throughout. Even the trills are slow: three of the five notes needed are already printed, and footnote (1) supplies the other two. In bar 17 they produce a note against note effect with the left hand that is easy to count. Although expressive, bar 21's dotted rhythm should be kept tightly rhythmical to produce a serious and impressively controlled finish.

Tone colour? Composer Arthur Benjamin (see below) arranged this and three other Cimarosa sonatas to form an oboe concerto with strings. As you may guess, the oboe leads almost throughout: first and second violins play the right-hand thirds in bars 5–8, the soloist then answering with the demisemi figures. Contrasted dynamics are in order here ('violins' f or p, 'oboe' the opposite). Bar 12 would be the ideal place for a brief cadenza, but without one it need not last the whole of its printed length: the near whole-bar silence was a grammatical requirement in an age which frowned on the odd bar of, say, $\frac{2}{4}$ amid the prevailing $\frac{4}{4}$.

Domenico Cimarosa, incidentally, led an eventful life, working in Naples, Rome, St Petersburg and Vienna, and composing, besides 200-odd keyboard sonata movements (possibly intended for playing in groups of two, three or four to form larger works), 60 operas, the most famous being *Il matrimonio segreto*, 'The Secret Marriage'. His death was bitterly tragic: he was arrested in 1799 and sentenced to death for pro-French revolutionary sympathies, but was reprieved and exiled from his then-home city (Naples). He departed for St Petersburg, and died on the journey.

Chopin	Valse KK IVb no. 11	Trinity Guildhall

One edition says this was composed in 1847, another 1843. Oddly, both could almost be right: Chopin was in the habit of rewriting compositions years later for friends and students. When doing this from memory, he would make slight alterations (or even misremember details), making life difficult for editors ever since: no such problem with this piece, where all sources match. Startlingly perhaps, this piece did not appear in print until 1955, when it was published in the French periodical *La Revue Musicale*. Sparse in texture and technically simple, it needs expressive awareness to avoid sounding dull. Chopin wrote no slurs in bars 9–16 but surely expected phrasing as in bars 1–8. Dynamics, too, are lacking: the overall mood suggests starting p – or else mf, optionally dropping to p at bar 9. Bars 17–24 could be played brighter and more brilliant than the start, even though staying in the minor – or, unexpectedly perhaps, making a ghostly pp in bars 21–24. The major-key passage (bars 33–40) is definitely an mf gap in the prevailing clouds, and could even go very slightly faster than the opening tempo. Try 'placing' bar 41's return to the minor with a *tenuto* beforehand; make a brief expressive swell in bar 51, and finish either p – tearfully – or mf – sorrowful but stoically dry-eyed. Memorisers beware: compare non-identical chords in bars 3 and 7, and 33 and 35 (the changes make for richer harmony); and notice that bar 25, unlike every other appearance of this theme, has no upbeat. Place right hand thumb on E's through bar 21, and get up to speed by practising (strictly in tempo) from the last E, then from the previous E, then from the beginning of the bar.

Fuchs	Lieb' Schwesterlein (Dear Little Sister) op. 32 no. 14	Trinity Guildhall

Like the Cimarosa (see above), this piece is easier than it looks, and (check the suggested metronome mark) probably goes twice as slowly as you first thought. There is plenty of time for even a small hand to negotiate the left-hand arpeggios, and for the right hand to balance each melody note so as to produce controlled phrasing without bumps. Robert Fuchs is little-known now (as is his elder brother, opera composer Johann Nepomuk Fuchs) but he taught, among others, Mahler, Sibelius and Hugo Wolf – and no less a figure than Brahms described him as 'a splendid musician; everything is so fine and so skilful, so charmingly invented, that one is always pleased.' At the correct (very slow) tempo, take care not to misread the last notes of bars 2, 3, 9, 10 and so on as quick upbeats: they are leisurely, *cantabile*, and of course are no shorter than the arpeggio notes they follow. Add warmth with pedal almost throughout, mostly in continuous crotchets (*legato* pedal if possible): change cleanly, and carefully finger-hold F♯s (right hand, bar 3; left hand, bars 13-14) to avoid losing notes as the pedal changes – though release bar 24's minim B if uncomfortable, letting the pedal sustain it. Strict tempo throughout would be the wrong style – try broadening out over barlines 4/5, 11/12, 12/13 and within bars 15, 21 ('placing' the D♯ after so much D♮) and 23, making expressive climaxes with unhurriedly spread chords where marked. Candidates with small hands could finish the right hand of bar 12 with 14 15 14. The German instruction *sehr langsam*, *innig Süss* may be translated as 'very slow, with inner sweetness.'

Bartók	Evening in the Country	Trinity Guildhall

This tuneful piece is perfect for anyone nervous of Bartók by reputation: nothing here is as ferocious as the *Allegro barbaro*, *The Miraculous Mandarin*, or the string quartets. Think of it as a folk song without words in three verses, accompanied by a village chorus coming in at a different place every time in the tune, and comprising medium voices for verse 1 (bar 1), deep men's voices for verse 2 (bar 21), then full chorus – with two solo voices this time, not just one – for verse 3 (bar 42). There is a dance interlude between verses: a flute solo with light off beat dance steps from bar 10, then piccolo with dance steps on every beat from bar 30. The dances stay in strict time and end abruptly (if Bartók had wanted a *rall.* he would have said so), but the verses are *rubato*, needing flexible tempo: for example, try hurrying the quavers ever so slightly in mid-phrase, then slowing down to end the first, second and fourth but (to avoid being predictable) not the third phrase. Notice the pauses after three phrases (but not the fourth) of verse 2. The melody is particularly passionate for verse 3: notice how the accompaniment is marked at a lower dynamic, and that the long melody notes will only sustain with careful pedalling. Resist the subconscious tendency to change pedal on every left-hand chord, and remember, when judging the pp in bar 53, that the last chord of the piece is ppp.

Benjamin	Silent and soft and slow descends the snow	Trinity Guildhall

Anglo-Australian composer Arthur Benjamin was a student of Stanford at the Royal College of Music and later taught there himself, his piano students including Benjamin Britten. His best-known piece has to be the *Jamaican Rumba*, one result of a passion for Caribbean and Latin-American music inspired by his visits there – as an examiner! Much of Benjamin's music is light and cheerful (for example, *From Santo Domingo* and *The Red River Jig*), but there is also a darkly serious post-war Symphony, and thoughtful works like this piano piece, composed in 1935.

Silent and Soft ... is a good introduction to *una corda* (the left pedal). If this is new to you, take care to avoid any middle pedal that may be present. Unlike the sustaining pedal, the *una corda* goes down (in advance) and stays down (without changing) until cancelled by *tre corde* (here, in bars 4 and 12). When performing on a real grand piano, be aware that (i) the whole keyboard will move sideways as the *una corda* pedal is pressed, and (ii) the change of tone colour may not be the same as on some electronic keyboards. *Una corda* thins out the tone, hence its abandonment for the lyrical *tre corde* passages. Both pedals go down in bar 35: remember to keep the left foot down while lifting the right foot for bar 36. Here and elsewhere, the sustaining pedal is carefully marked: it fills bar 8 despite the printed rests, and using it on single notes (in bars like 24) adds warmth. Check left-hand ties and slurs in bars like 5–6. Release the left hand smartly from bars 9 and 17 to enable the same pitches in the other hand to respond. The final theme continues beyond the printed slur (bars 33-34) through to bar 35, without losing the tension.

Krebs	Wer nur den lieben Gott lässt walten	
	(from *The Age of J S Bach* – Intermediate Piano Book)	Peters

Johann Ludwig Krebs (1713-1780) was a student of J S Bach, whose own Cantata no. 93 has this same title (the opening line of a seventeenth-century hymn meaning 'Whoever lets beloved God do his work'). This prelude on the hymn tune is obviously suited to the organ (Krebs's own instrument) though effective on piano if played seriously and smoothly, never percussive even when marked *ff*.

Mordents on or just after quavers may be played as follows:

Bars 1, 2, 3, 7, 8 Bars 4, 5   *or* (easier)   Bars 1, 7, 8   Bars 2,3   Bars 4,5

– but those amid semiquaver runs (bars 6-7) may be reduced to single grace notes (above the printed note) or omitted altogether, to avoid dragging the whole tempo much below ♩ = 66. Small hands may break before the top notes of bars 4, 5 and 10, while hands of all sizes should lift punctually in bars 13-14 for seamlessly joined hand-to-hand semiquavers. Bar 16's trill is eight demisemiquavers, starting on the upper note and ending with the two printed. Low E here is tied, of course, this whole bar broadening and, on piano or harpsichord, the last left-hand chord optionally arpeggiated.

Grieg	Waltz op. 38 no. 7 (from *Lyric Pieces* book 2)	Henle *or* Peters

Basically simple though with some unexpected harmonies, this needs expressive right-hand shading at cadences, delicacy and agility in the central *Presto*, and a critical eye for some potentially messy printed pedallings for which Grieg (or his first publisher) was notorious. Left-hand skips of a tenth, however, may all be managed through hop-and-pedal (bars 5-6, 9-10) or with rolled arm (bar 24).

Carefully *dim.* (even though not printed) in the right hand in bars 7-8, 15-16 (where you may take the tenor A in the right hand) and even more carefully in slower bars 52-53. Left-hand slurs (not ties) in each bar from 17-20 imply similar 'strong-weak' shading. Lift bar 9's pedal on the second crotchet, *simile* in bar 10; change on 3rd, 4th and 5th crotchets of bars 13-14. Lift the left hand while sustaining the right in bar 32, before the quasi-improvisatory cadenza: the reprise from bar 38 is not exact, bar 41's harmony being different, as are the dynamics around it. The syllable-by-syllable *ritardando* printed in bars 11-16 should be less than that in bars 48-52, which reaches a distinctly slower speed.

Lutosławski	Inwencja (Invention) (from *The Most Beautiful Lutosławski*)	PWM

Witold Lutosławski (1913-1994) was one of Poland's best-loved and most respected post-war composers. This two-part Invention of 1968 is ideal for small hands. Don't be put off by the constantly changing time signatures: ♪ = ♪ throughout, and the pulse never stops. More tricky is the very chromatic, not-quite-tonal idiom, hard to absorb and its pitches hard to check in performance. Both rhythm and tonality are influenced by Bartók, Lutosławski developing short phrases by expansion, contraction and inexact inversion. For example, the right-hand three-crotchet falling semitone figure in bars 3-4 speeds up in bars 9 and 11 (with a falling fourth), 17, 20 and the end of 21 (here with a falling whole tone) and returns to normal in bars 26-27. Bars 17-19 (right hand) contract over barline 21/22; bars 28-31 summarise the pitches of bars 1-9, and left hand of bars 31-33 (complete with grammatical but odd-looking A♯-B♭ tie) contract straight away (where A♯-B♭ looks even odder: just hold an A♯ crotchet here), resolving onto a D as if the most logical cadence in the world.

Advanced Level

At Advanced level (Grades 6-8), candidates will typically be able consciously to integrate their skills, knowledge and understanding in a secure and sustained performance which demonstrates mature grasp of the material. Along with confidence, a sense of ownership and self-awareness, this will result in a discriminating and sensitive personal interpretation that conveys complexity and control of shape (e.g. throughout a sonata movement), and awareness of stylistic interpretation. The performance will be grounded in thorough and relevant preparation and will demonstrate authority and control. Candidates will combine skilful and appropriate command with imaginative response and flair to engage the audience wholeheartedly.

These features will be demonstrated through material largely drawn from the standard repertoire for the instrument. Overall length will be sufficient to enable variety and range of presentation to be demonstrated and sustained. Content will be substantial, with some depth and sophistication, enabling the candidate to engage with complex emotions and abstract musical thought. It will be such as to require analysis and reflection in the preparation, and present challenging physical requirements in one or more technical aspects. The musical language may demand considerable inferential understanding and thoughtful interpretation to reflect subtlety of meaning (e.g. contrapuntal texture; musical irony or humour).

Grade 6

Group A

Telemann	**Fantasia in F, TWV 33:5**	**Trinity Guildhall**

Telemann not only lived to a ripe old age for a man of his generation, but composed almost continuously throughout his life time. The statistics are astounding: over 1,000 church cantatas and more than 50 secular ones; 46 complete settings of the Passion story (one per year, 1722-1767); 17 operas; oratorios and masses; orchestral overtures (i.e. multi-movement suites) and nearly 1,000 concertos; over 150 keyboard pieces. This Fantasia may remind you of Handel's famous Fantasia in C, properly so since it comes from a set of 'Thrice Twelve Fantasias' deliberately composed in French, Italian and (as here) German styles. The *Allegro* originally came first, then the Largo, plus a *da capo* to allow the whole *Allegro* again. The alternative layout here works just as well.

The Lento is brief but weighty and serious. Count a steady six-in-the-bar, noticing that footnoted ornament (1) stops just before the count of '2' – one of several beats in this section where nothing actually plays. Bar 4's trill starts on the upper note (G) and comprises four demisemiquavers. Finger the end of footnote (2)'s trill with 3 and 4 to prepare for the following chord, which may be arpeggiated (even though not so marked) for a stately finish. The changes of chord throughout bars 1-4 may also be arpeggiated, to highlight the harmonic progression. Bring off all notes punctually before rests, and phrase smoothly right up to bar 9, where the lower right-hand A (try f from here, after a possible p at bar 4/5 and f at the beginning) may detach to highlight the octave leap: the following left hand may imitate it.

Dynamics must be varied: the *Allegro* in particular would be very dull all at the same level. Possible echoes may start at bars 14, 30 and 51/52. Other clues are internal: high-pitched and active music may be *f* (bars 12, 15/6, 27/8, 39), while sequences may start *p* (21/22, 24/25 – control the left hand from here with practice-accents on every beat – 45/46, 48). Other passages may be *p* to contrast with the general extroversion (bars 30/31, 37/38 – try starting a *cresc.* from here), to bring out fleeting pathos (the chromatics in bar 41) or to underline a change of mode (bar 35). Repeated quavers may well all be *staccato*; stepwise 'walking' bass *legato*, varied with *staccato* octave leaps from bar 16. Check for F♯s through bars 23-24, and ensure that the snappy two-demisemi one-semi flourishes in bars 15-17 – and particularly 36-38 – never degenerate into triplets.

J S Bach	Gigue (from English Suite no. 2 BWV 807)	Trinity Guildhall

J S Bach and Telemann famously competed for the job of Cantor at St Thomas' Church, Leipzig. Telemann was first choice but declined, the authorities reluctantly employing Bach instead. Both men wrote a prodigious amount (Bach in a shorter lifetime), this Gigue being the 7th movement from one of no less than six English Suites, grander in design than the French Suites sampled in Grade 5.

Brush up on trills (in both hands!) for the eventual speed in this piece depends on well-articulated ornaments (cropping up as unnervingly early as bars 7, 9 and 11) and wide left-hand leaps (over barlines 22/23 and 24/25). The left hand is often tricky: consider practising it alone in bars 28-35 and from 52 right through to 65. Perversely, the 'easy' key of A minor, with its almost total lack of hand-position-friendly black notes, can be hard to finger confidently. Learn fingerings securely, particularly in contrary motion passages like bars 17-20 and 40-51 and in that delightful passage from bar 30 (and 69) where the left hand rises through 2-and-a-half octaves, seeming to chase the right hand like a pair of butterflies on the wing. There are few obvious places to drop to *p* after an initial *f*, but contrast is needed somewhere – possibly from bar 21 (ditto 61), with a *cresc.* through the 'chase' passages. Try a long *dim.* to *pp* during the ever-descending bars 39-46 – inauthentic, possibly, but it would certainly add to the drama. In a concert performance playing all the necessary links and repeats as printed would make this Gigue rather long. In the exam, omit the *D.S.* and all repeats, and go straight from bar 73 to the *Fine* bar, fingering left hand 2/5 over barline 73/74.

Mozart	Sonata in C, K. 330, 2nd movement: Andante cantabile	Trinity Guildhall

This piece is Mozart in tenderest mode, reaching tragedy in the minor section though always within the bounds of good 18th-century taste, and at an unhurried pace hinting at vast spaces which in practice makes even a quaver last a long time, and a crotchet feel almost static.

Pencil-in six quaver counts per bar, not neglecting the footnotes. Count '2' of the six is often crucial: ornament (1) turns just before it, trill (3) halts on it, right-hand demisemis in bars 3 and 5 move after (not on) it, and nothing at all moves on it in any even-numbered bar up to 18, nor in bars 9 or 17. (Double-check the bar numbering: some bars are split over two systems.) Beware: bar 6's high G holds longer than bar 5's, the demisemiquavers in bar 6 moving after '3' and the top C coming on '4'. Hold alto F while releasing the left-hand chord in bar 11, and release the left hand punctually in bar 26 to leave the right hand hanging unaccompanied before moving off. Small notes above the main note, as in bars 8 and 11, go as per footnote – but those below, namely in bar 25, may go differently, as single demisemis on the beat, the D♭s therefore becoming dotted semis after it.

Whatever the prevailing dynamic, remember that p and f were not as extreme on Mozart's instruments as they are now. fs are warm, never hard, and contrasts between them and *pianos* need not always be abrupt: in fact bar 6 would sound absurd if suddenly dropping to p on its high note. Fingerings: try left hand 12 13 124 to close bar 10 if in trouble; delay bar 13's finger-changing 1–2 until after the high G. Apply footnote (2) to bar 11, noticing that the small C♮ will now sound on the count of '6' together with alto and bass. The B♭ sounds alone, afterwards. Similar dislocations also occur in bars 24 and 35. The first three repeated quavers of the whole piece (similarly elsewhere) are warm and possibly pedalled. From bar 21 you have a choice: pedalling the left-hand semis add warmth while unpedalled ones conjure up a desolate string-quartet sound: your choice. The left hand is as expressive as the right hand from bar 29, a four-bar love duet. The anguished discord at bar 39 is still within pp – a pin-prick, not a blow to the solar plexus. Bars 40/41–60 beat 2 exactly repeat bars 0/1–20 beat 2, while *coda*-bars 60 (last three quavers)–64 neatly reuse the minor episode codetta bars 36 (last three quavers)–40.

Burgmüller	Morning Bells op. 109 no. 9	Trinity Guildhall

The New Grove Dictionary has been rather uncomplimentary about Friedrich Burgmüller, suggesting his short-lived younger brother Norbert was a composer with greater promise. Their father, Johann Augustus Franz, was musical director of a theatre, something that may have inspired son Friedrich to compose the ballet *La Péri* while in Paris, a score that impressed no less a judge than Berlioz.

'Our' Burgmüller is probably best known today for his piano studies, and their quality may be fairly judged by this (or rather, these) *Morning Bells*, which ping charmingly through bars 1–8 and 25–34. Land gently on them as you cross hands: this is part of the technical study, as is the shaping of the treble melody (bringing out each note above subdued alto quavers is just the first step), then you should project not just one but two melodies in bars 9–16 (one deliberately fainter than the other) above an accompaniment that must stay gentle despite some wide skips – to which you should add suitable pedal, say a two-bar pattern of minim–crotchet crotchet–minim. (Pedalling skills will be warmed up in bars 1–7, say with a minim–crotchet pattern.) Broaden out, even without being asked, towards – and through – bar 17's climax. Some editions have bass A♭ here, unwilling to believe the striking dissonance that (correct) C makes with treble D♭. Bars 21–24 are not mere decoration but an operatic coloratura (more theatrical influence, maybe), ranging far wider than any singer could possibly go, and *molto cantabile* throughout: check the switch from *legato* to *staccato*, and the exact note lengths in the accompaniment. Make all the spreads deliberate, even though easily within reach (bars 6, 11, 13, 17, 18, 30) – they are expressive emphases – and try ending the whole piece with a big *rit.*, possibly pedalling each quaver separately from the end of bar 35.

Scarlatti	Sonata in G, K. 2	
	(p. 78 from *Schott Piano Collection – D Scarlatti*)	Schott

In binary form, like most of Domenico Scarlatti's sonatas, this extrovert piece is easier once past the arpeggios of bars 3-4 (worth practising in dotted rhythms). Dynamic contrasts are mostly abrupt, ideally suiting the two-manual harpsichord for which it was originally written – but it could all be orchestrated like a concerto grosso. Imagine two trumpets at bars 5 and 9 (horns at equivalent bars 42 and 46), one trumpet at 21, the other at 25, two flutes at 13, two violins at 15 and 19, two oboes at 17 (and 50), the whole concertino section at 29, the *ripieno* at bars 7, 11, 23, 27 and 33, everyone together for bars 1-4 and 35-37, and so on.

The second half is not an exact reprise of the first, bars 50-53 being in minor, not major as before (bars 13-16); bars 58-61 are inserted between the equivalent of bars 20 and 21; bar 63 jumps an octave, not a fifth, and bar 70's octave displacement forces a leap for both hands that will need practise. The last right-hand note of each half is effective with an added mordent, which can be prolonged into a trill to close the whole piece.

Paradies	Toccata in A (from *Baroque Real Repertoire*)	Trinity Faber

Probably the only piece of Domenico Paradies that most people know, this Toccata is its sonata's second movement. Check the edition: the second 16-semiquaver phrase should match the first (ditto after the repeat mark) and the total bar-count should be 80. Most editions conform, though one or two, for no doubt scholarly though unfathomable reasons, omit the second phrase entirely, which throws the phrase-structure awry.

Unnervingly perhaps, the opening semiquavers switch direction from descending to ascending pairs – thereafter things run more smoothly, just requiring neat, controlled and almost entirely unpedalled playing, with careful reading of final (unpredictable) semiquavers in bars 12-19 (and equivalent bars 64-71) and extra right-hand practice of bars 50-53. Dynamic changes (none suggested) should be distinct yet not exaggerated, and may go thus: *f* to start, then at bars 6 (halfway through), 12, 24, 28, 34 (halfway through), 52 and halfway through the following bars: 56, 60, 62, 74 and 78; *p* halfway through bars 2, 12, 16, 21, 24, 30, 44, 50, 52, 58, 61, 73 and 77 and on fourth quavers of bars 8, 36 and 40; bars 4 (halfway through), 16, 20, 32 (halfway through), 40, 44 and 48 may be *mp* or *mf*; and try *cresc.* through bars 5, 11, 15, 19, 23, 27, 33, 39, 43, 47, 51 and 56. Bars 64 onwards may copy bar 12, or – bearing in mind this is a triumphant sprint in the home key – may stay *f*, and the last chord of each half may be spread.

J C Bach	Sonata in B♭, op. 5 no. 1, 1st movement: Allegretto	
	(from *Piano Sonatas* vol. I)	Henle

J C Bach is often nicknamed the 'London' Bach on account of his work there – but the name 'Mozart' Bach might be more suitable, for his style is far-removed from that of father J S and much influenced the young Mozart. Neat melodies and controlled Alberti basses are common to both composers, plus an air of unruffled good manners: this sonata movement is plastered with trills difficult to describe exhaustively in the available space. The following are textbook solutions, but may all be simplified if too awkward at normal speed ($\flat$ = 144).

- Regular demisemiquavers, starting on the upper note: bars 9, 11, 14, and halfway through bars 21, 29 and 43
- Demis incorporating a triplet, to end on the right pitch: 3, 8, 21, 29, 42 (starting on principal note); 16, 18, 24, 26 (starting on upper note)
- Hemidemis, starting on upper note (alternatively, omitted or replaced by before-the-beat grace notes): bars 0(/1), 34(/35), 38
- Bars 47–49: semi, demi triplet (the first being tied to previous semi), quaver or semi, two demis, quaver
- Grace notes in bars 15, 17 23, 25 are single demis on the beat; those in bars 4, 13, 57, 59 may (perhaps should) go before the beat

The printed dynamics may be supplemented as follows: start anywhere between *p* and *f*, though keeping the ornament light (same at 34/35); *cresc./dim.* in bars 3/4, similarly (*poco*) round barline 15/16 and (*più*) round 17/18 (23-26 *simile*); *cresc.* for bar 10's high-note variation; *dim.* in 14; *rinforzando* in 49, *molto f* at 55's dramatic diminished 7th. Short-long pairs of notes from bars 30 (*f*) and 32 (*p*) fit the repeated word 'steady!' or 'hiccup!', and are known as Scotch snaps. Approach bar 62 with *rall.* and *marcato* non-*legato* semis; try decorating the pause with a long trill and Adagio afterbeats. Memorisers should note two changes in the recapitulation: bar 22's octave displacement is now ironed out, and bar 77 adds a triplet.

Schumann	Erinnerung op. 68 no. 28 (from *Real Repertoire*)	Trinity Faber

This 'Remembrance' in memory of Mendelssohn may be for youngsters but its heartfelt appeal is for players of any age. There are few notes to learn, for bars 11-20 exactly repeat bars 1-10 and bars 33-44 repeat bars 21-32: in fact your edition may even use repeat marks to save space. If this is the case (i) read our bracketed alternative bar numbers, and (ii) play the repeats in the exam! Tenderness is required, besides a natural balance between tune and accompaniment that instinctively hushes bar 8's alto semiquavers beneath a fast-decaying melody note, doing the same in 32 yet still managing an internal suspension-and-resolution *dim.* Crotchet–quaver phrases in bars 2 and 6 should instinctively be shaded off; bar 5's turn starts on G♯, simultaneous with (not before) lower B and D♯, and bar 9's turn includes a G𝄪. Bar 24 (14)'s hands synchronise (after the gentlest left-hand offbeats) on fourth quaver, bar 31 (21)'s on third. Observe both pauses in bar 30 (20). More subtly, linger over bar 3's *cresc./dim.*, and emphasise the unusual six-bar phrasing thereafter by gently hurrying through bar 7 yet lingering in bar 9. Most subtly, imagine the overlapping phrases of bars 21-23 (11-13) as successive entries on clarinet, oboe and violins.

Chopin	Mazurka op. 24 no. 1 in G minor (from *Mazurkas*)	Henle *or* Peters

The mazurka was a patriotic Polish dance and can imply a basically strict tempo, though the second section (here, from bar 17) traditionally goes a little faster. Within this restrictive format Chopin covers a remarkable range of moods – gloom, yearning and wild abandon – and careful *rubato* can enhance them. Check the bar-count: we number first- and second-time bars as 32a and 32b, so the final bar is 64. This Mazurka requires careful reading (and memorising, if you dare) of similar but non-identical rhythms: compare bar 9 with 1, and 15 with 7; dotted quavers versus semiquaver rests in 33 and 39, 37 and 38; and the three different rhythms in bar 57 alone. More subtly, notice that there no dots in bar 5 (compare with bar 1).

Pedal markings are at odds with, and should often override (and fill), printed rests (bars 1, 5, 33-36, 41-44, 53, 57, 61), but not always: bars 3, 7, 11, 38, 46, possibly 49 and probably 62 are more effective if the rests, however tiny, are completely silent. Bar 8's grace note goes on the beat, 43's on or before (you choose). The left-hand stretches beyond an octave may be shared with the right hand, though bar 20's sweep is dramatic with rolled left arm. Bar 57's dot after the right-hand D applies only to sustained alto: unison treble D is just a quaver.

| Reinecke | Sonatine in A minor, op. 98 no. 2, 1st movement: Moderato | |
| | (from *Bärenreiter Sonatina Album* vol. 2) | Bärenreiter |

German composer Carl Reinecke (1824-1910) composed vast quantities of easy-going, eager-to-please though not always easy-to-play music – accompanists may recall his tricky half-hour flute sonata 'Undine'. This Sonatina movement may inadvertently remind jazz-lovers of *Nature Boy* (itself lifted from the Dvořák Piano Quintet) though Reinecke is strictly classical, characteristically repeating the same rhythms almost to excess and rarely becoming exciting until bars 88-92 (make the left hand *pesante* here). *Moderato* (not *Allegro*) may equate to ♩ = 96, a good starting tempo though it could increase for the second subject (bar 24 – left hand solo, right hand accompaniment, of course) and stay faster until bar 70. The second-subject recapitulation at bar 96, however, could well be closer to the starting tempo as part of a calming-down in proportion to a fairly long piece. The whole movement should certainly not end faster than it began. Don't neglect left-hand durations while busy with the right: this piece tests sustained right hand over often simultaneously lifted left. In performance with the repeat, bar 50-51's *cresc.* would be sudden; without the repeat (or on the second time), it is gradual, continuing through the second-time bar to a later *f*. Chord voicings in bars 52a and 124 are both odd and may stay unmatched.

| Ilyinsky | Berceuse op. 13 no. 7 (from *Romantic Real Repertoire*) | Trinity Faber |

Alexander Ilyinsky (1859-1920) taught at the Moscow Conservatoire, and is best-known for an opera named after a famous Russian tourist spot, *The Fountain of Bakhchisaray*. His Berceuse best suits players at ease in six flats, and with big hands: there are eleven spread tenths between bars 10 and 18, though they can all be broken provided the bass notes are caught with (split-second) pedal.

The opening pentatonic melody exudes calm, but the relative-minor episode from bar 11 is agitated and could go markedly faster than Tempo I, right up to bar 19, optionally returning to tempo not just where marked (22-23) but also (*poco a poco*) through 20-21. The ever-decreasing dynamics marked in bars 29-37 are optimistic if not impractical: play *mp* at 30/31 and 31/32, *p* at 33 (softer downbeat than upbeat), same at 34, *dim.* as marked in 34, and add *una corda* from 35 to the end. The footnoted on-the-beat acciaccatura occurs – easily overlooked – in bar 19. Editorial pedal marks are good, though they can be altered: bar 14 may go unpedalled, while bars 35-37 may equally be taken in one unchanged 2½-bar pedal. The final chord may be played with LLRRL as suggested (a pleasing visual effect), though players nervous of hand-crossing may arpeggiate more slowly, left-hand 5-1-2 being followed by RR.

Group B

Granados   Vals Noble (no. 2 of *Valses poéticos*)   Trinity Guildhall

Isaac Albeniz and Enrique Granados were the giants of Romantic Spanish piano music despite their almost equally short lives. Both men died around the age of 48, Granados tragically in World War I: the ship in which he was travelling to America was torpedoed and although he survived the initial impact, he drowned trying to save his wife from the wreckage.

Some of Granados' music (notably the Goya-inspired piano series *Goyescas*) is fiendishly elaborate and the pages black with notes: not so this early waltz, which is simple and plumbs few emotional depths. Bring out the melody, of course, then shape it – easy to do at the start where rotated left arm (with 2nd finger as a pivot) will keep the wide-stretched arpeggios quiet and controlled, a little trickier when quicker (and sustained almost unpedalled over *staccato* figures) from bar 17. Granados asks for *rubato* in bars 7, 23 and 53 (try lingering over the first three quavers each time) and *con molto fantasia* in bars 13 and 59 (try lingering even longer). Take last note of bar 20 with left hand if nervous of mis-hitting that top F. Pedal wherever there are no *staccato* marks – except at bar 30, where the two-note calls sound better if kept clear. Start the piece with whole-bar pedals (the same whenever long bass notes need to be held, e.g. bars 31-32 and 63-64), then let your ear tell you where you need to change more often: probably minim-crotchet in bars 8 and 14, and minim-nothing in bars 9-12. Don't short change the printed pauses in bars 16, 32 and 64; observe the printed *rits* and experiment with an added *rit*. in bar 48.

Khachaturian   Legend (from *Pictures of Childhood*)   Trinity Guildhall

Most pieces for children are cheerful, gentle and generally lightweight. Here, by contrast, is a deeply serious piece, recalling the gloomy world of Dostoyevsky. Those straining *crescs* in bars 1-2 lead to a G minor resting-point (bar 4, distorted by unpedalled and off-colour bass notes) through strange dissonances. Read bar 3 very carefully (repeated in bars 7, 29 and 32) and prepare to remain puzzled by the harmony. Bars 9-14 are plaintive and nagging, bars 15-16 anguished, 19-22 plunging despairingly to a reprise wearily dragged down a semitone from the original key to an F# minor reprise from bar 23, then crying out f in high C minor (bar 26) before finding G minor again (bar 30), this time with unexpected changes of dynamic. Bar 4's off-colour bass roughly inverts in bar 33, and bar 35's climactic G minor chord is dramatically soured by an F#. Technically, notice bar 3's (and 32's) bass G, still natural amid all those flats; crossed hands (of course) in bar 9; Eb through bar 16 and C# through bars 18-19. Try minim-crotchet pedals in bars 1-3 and 5-7, then little if any pedal until bar 22. Spiritually, if you like this piece and want to explore further, track down the complete *Pictures* and sample *A Glimpse of the Ballet* (extremely sparse, but very expressive), then lighten up with the *Toccata* and the *Folk Dance* from the same collection.

| Agay | Ballad Improvisation | Trinity Guildhall |

The *Joy Of Boogie And Blues*, from which this piece comes, was part of a vast *Joy Of* series that Hungarian-born Denes Agay patiently compiled over a very long lifetime (1911–2007). *Ballad* (in the jazz sense) is a very accurate title: the notes of this reflective piece are very easy, and the skill lies in careful manipulation of tempo so as to move freely (as requested), convincingly, and without too much rhythmic distortion. Strict tempo scarcely applies, save perhaps for bars 5–6 and 13–14, which could be called 'control' bars (in the scientific-experiment sense) that re-establish the basic pulse before it spins freely once more. The 'growing excitement' requested in bar 17 should spread over four bars and not peak too soon; bar 22's sostenuto may be read as *poco rit.*, a more noticeable *rit.* occurring at 24. The opening tune resumes from bar 25, spread over a wider range: maintain an unbroken phrase as you cross hands rather than draw attention to the separate printed slurs. *Dim.* only slightly towards bar 32, for there are three more reductions of volume still to come. See how far you can get without using the pedal, and try playing the very last (D major) chord slightly late, and with mystery, to avoid it sounding corny.

| McCabe | Forlane (from *Afternoons and Afterwards*) | Trinity Guildhall |

A Forlane is a kind of barcarolle (think Venetian gondoliers), with a typical lilting $^6_8$ pulse. Probably its most famous example is in Ravel's suite *Le Tombeau de Couperin*, a piece that British composer John McCabe must have been fully aware of, for he almost quotes it in bars 22–31, inventing cadence chords quite as juicy as, if completely different from, Ravel's own. The opening sequence of major seconds place it firmly up-to-date (the component notes should synchronise exactly, whatever their fingering, for a convincing start) before the music settles into what is actually (despite the lack of key signature) C# minor. Be *cantabile* (but not forceful) from bar 4, not easy in such a high thin register: notice a half-hidden change of harmony in bar 8 and some subtle desynchronisations between the hands thereafter. Bar 11 contains G naturals, easily missed after so many preceding G#s; bar 29 likewise contains easy-to-miss F♮s while a common sight-reading trap lies in wait at bar 30 – top notes are D♭ and E, not D and E♭. The reprise (from bar 32) is cleverly telescoped; bar 39's long and unchanged pedal is vital, for the whole chord should still be reverberating at bar 41. Dynamics here remind you to peal out the final phrase, *mf* after that *pp* chord which would sound so effective on a vibraphone.

| Lane | Private Detective | Trinity Guildhall |

The irresistible 'New York, New York' introduction may tempt you to invoke the swagger of all those 1940s film heroes. But look at the very quick metronome mark: even if you can't quite reach it, this piece is bright and sassy, more Kinsey Milhone than Philip Marlowe. This is swing, of course, where dotted quaver–semiquaver rhythms and paired quavers (the second tied to the following note, as in bars 5, 7 and 9) slacken quite legitimately into triplets (imagine them written as crotchet-plus-quaver beneath a triplet sign). Notice the change of clef and crossed hands at bar 5: imagine a solo trombone (right hand) and banjo (high left hand), followed by muted jazz trumpet (answered by high clarinet) from bar 15. The *glissando* at bar 20 should startle: both here and in bar 28 hold the hand at an angle and keep it high so that the keys strike the nail, not the skin, otherwise it will hurt! In each case, stop a fraction early so as to prepare the following downbeat accurately, covering the gap with pedal, which if applied throughout will make both *glissandi*s sound infinitely more spectacular, staccato chords at bar 28 notwithstanding. Accented 'big band' crotchet chords in bars 31–37 (plus the marked crotchet in bar 43, and, much earlier, the second note of bar 16) should be swung, i.e. delayed, like those paired quavers mentioned earlier: dynamics are sparse in this piece but this passage can surely go *f* or even *ff*. Come off punctually before bar 44, and play the very last bass flicker (after, say, three extra crotchets'-worth of pause) like a drummer making a cut-off.

Skryabin	Prelude no. 21 in B♭ (from *24 Preludes* op. 11)	Henle

Alexander Skryabin (1872–1915) eventually became notorious as a megalomaniac mystic, composing massive orchestral works like the *Poem of Ecstasy* and *Prometheus, Poem of Fire*, and (for piano) ten sonatas, all fearsomely difficult to play – yet his early works contain dozens of intimate miniatures whose main challenge is not technical but interpretative. He was much influenced by Chopin and demands a similar awareness of *rubato* and the psychology of particular chord progressions. This Prelude features slow but hugely extended left-hand arpeggios that require relaxed lateral arm movement to keep them much softer than a right-hand melody, which is itself gentle and unforced. Balance is particularly crucial in bars like 4 and 8, where the left hand must tail away to *ppp* to avoid overwhelming fast-decaying melody notes less than an octave above.

Yes, a miniature: yet the main melody, disjointed-sounding at first hearing even when properly pedalled (i.e. more or less continuously, without blurring different harmonies or filling brief silences), completes two vast twelve-bar spans hinting at far horizons. Skyrabin left few dynamics: start *p*, play *mp* from bar 5 and *mf* from bar 9; *p* again at 13 and *mp* at 17, thereafter as printed, bearing in mind that – although few editions show it – Skryabin later added '*p* e *rit*.' to bar 12 and delayed bar 25's *pp* by two beats. He also added *tenuto* marks to bar 12's first four left-hand quavers, and another *rit*. in bar 24. The Henle edition has (probably correctly) an E♮ in bar 10, flattened in bar 11 – and (less certainly) a dotted minim and no *dim*. in bar 16, unlike the analogous bar 4 which has *dim*. and dotted semibreve. This is fragile music, needing delicate and sympathetic handling.

Ibert	A Giddy Girl (from *4 pièces célèbres, extraites des 'Histoires'*)	Leduc

Jacques Ibert (1890–1962), possibly best-known for his riotous *Divertissement* for small orchestra, wrote his ten *Histoires* in 1931 – the best-known is *Le petit âne blanc* ('The Little White Donkey'). Like Debussy *Préludes* their titles appear only at the end of each piece.

As the French instruction suggests, this piece pokes gentle fun at Englishness, and although marked *Allant* (literally 'going', i.e. *con moto*) should not exceed around ♩ = 96. There is no distinct 'tune and accompaniment' at first, tenor and soprano being equally expressive in bars 3–4 and more so (with wider *cresc./dim*.) in higher-pitched 7–8. Compare the unaccompanied 'ping!' that closes bar 4 with the paused one (over held chord) in 8; distinguish light-hearted *staccato* quavers in 1–2 and 5–6 from *tenuto* ones in sombre and slower bars 9–14. It's hard to 'exaggerate the nuances (light-and-shade)' as requested in bars 17–18 where none are signalled: maybe the slurring needs underlining. Alto C𝄪 and D♮ here are of course the same note, tied. Elsewhere, read carefully bar 9's G minor chord and bar 13's E7; bar 12's treble semiquaver is still G♯ and tenor's quaver still A♯ (the *sf* here is a stab of anxiety). Any tied-over treble F♯ at the beginning of bar 16 is a misprint and the note should be deleted: the bar starts with treble C♯ crotchet over tied lower voices. Semiquavers in bars 19–24 are not triplets; don't hurry bar 26; and draw out the close as the hand-crossing 'pings' resolve up the scale.

Arnold	The Buccaneer	
	(from *Twentieth Century Real Repertoire*)	Trinity Faber

For this gloriously unsubtle piece, think Bluto from Popeye: a grossly fat, thickly bearded pirate, with a bellowing laugh, a bone-crushing handshake, and a filthy jersey stinking of fish, tobacco and gallons of spilt rum. Malcolm Arnold, for many years a trumpeter in the London Philharmonic Orchestra, wrote much film music, and many of his concert works sound like film scores too: the oom pahs in bars 7-12 are typical, and his harmony often settles contentedly on alternating chords, like the Bm+^{7}/Am+^{7} of bars 9-10, the Fb^{10}/Em^9 of bars 13-14 (all identical with his Clarinet Sonatina composed around the same time, the 1950s) and the opening C+^{7}/D9+^{5} which keeps him happy for the first six bars. ♪ = ♪ throughout: if in trouble, compare bar 11's and 17's cross-rhythm crotchets with how they fit over bar 20's bass, and/or imagine the second crotchet notated as ♪ ♪ . Sudden ***pp***s are also part of Arnold's style, and the single suspended note over bar 28's detached bass (difficult to practise without pedal because of the page turn) should sound spooky. Bars 29-33 remain ***pp***, though their music was originally loud. The final leap is tricky: memorise, and watch your hands.

Brubeck	A Misty Morning (from *Nocturnes*)	Warner Bros

Jazz pianist Dave Brubeck (born 1920) is famous for exuberant pieces in unusual time signatures like *Blue Rondo à la Turk*, *Eleven-Four* and, most famously, *Take Five*. Forget all of those here: this nocturne is deeply gloomy. Its mood and subtitle ('So This is Kirsten' – a phrase incidentally fitting the first five notes) sound as if whoever's meeting Kirsten doesn't like her at all. The piece is an exercise in bringing out a middle-register melody and subduing big-looking but very gentle chords. Check the bar-count: we number first- and second-time bars separately, the second-time bar being 14 and the first *coda*-bar 24.

The opening pedal mark sounds blurred but is necessary to match the same phrase later, whose accompanimental chords cannot be sustained by fingers alone and – as in Debussy – must be held with pedal according to the longest printed note. Unlike Debussy's usage, paired diagonal slashes signify cut offs and silent pauses: slight in bar 13 and longer in 23. Middle-section harmonies are juicy but the melody can drag if in strict tempo: try pushing onwards, then make a *poco rit.* in 20-21 and *più rit.* in 22-23. Mysteriously, the mode switches to major for the final bar, 'placed' at leisure though specifically, if curiously, not repedalled.

Grade 7
Group A

| Rameau | L'Egiptienne | | Trinity Guildhall |

French Baroque composer Jean-Philippe Rameau composed vast quantities of keyboard pieces, giving many of them pictorial or fanciful titles. He was also a great composer for the theatre, many of his operas being remarkably adventurous for their time and once or twice even straying beyond the technical capabilities of the orchestral instruments. No such problem with *L'Egiptienne*, where the main challenge may be to negotiate the thicket of ornaments, typical of the time. The album footnotes help with the decoding, but even then some bars will sound quite different from the way they look, and it may be worth writing out what you will actually play in the right hand of bars 21-26. Notice yet another ornament (in bar 65) when this music recurs at bars 63-66 – and compare bar 42 with (suitably transposed) footnote 1, the alto B♭ therefore synchronising with the fourth actual note in the soprano, and the whole thing being fingered 3 4 3 24. Bar 60's ornaments have all occurred before: the first goes like footnote (4) and the second like footnote (3).

Dynamics, in music of this style, may be deduced from internal clues. This is harpsichord music (on which instrument, given two manuals, the crossed-hands opening would be a lot less awkward than on piano), so expect most dynamics to be terraced – that is, with clear changes between *f* and *p* – though a few *crescendos* may not be inappropriate. Try starting *f*, dropping to *p* at the chirruping bar 10/11 (the call of a Nile water bird, maybe – or even a frog?). Try *f* at bar 17 and *p* at the obvious echo place (19), ditto *f* at 22/23 (approached by an optional *cresc.*), *p* at 24/25, and either *f* again at 26/27 or else *p* then *cresc.* through 28-29 to *f* at 30. Notice how bar 70 varies slightly from equivalent bar 30, presumably to stay within the available compass. Like Bach (often), Rameau lands on a firm tonic (bar 32) and ruminates gently over a tonic pedal point. The final chord of each half (bars 36 and 76) may be approached *cresc.* and be legitimately arpeggiated for a convincing signing off. Many similar patterns recur in the second half, and can use similar dynamics.

| Scarlatti | Sonata in E, K. 380 | | Trinity Guildhall |

Everyone knows that Scarlatti wrote his 555 or so sonatas for a two-manual harpsichord, which probably had more than just two tone colours: there could be extra stops for brightness (4-foot) and depth (16-foot), plus a novelty stop (the 'lute') which provided a stifled and barely reverberating *staccato*. Think colourfully, therefore, and in this sonata you may even imagine not just harpsichord but orchestral sounds: flutes or oboes in bars 1-4, for instance (depending on whether you choose to start *p* or *f*), horns in bars 5-8, trumpets in bars like 19 and 21 (answered by horns again, a bar later), violins from bar 36, and even a strummed guitar in the left-hand chords (some of which you may arpeggiate) from bar 12. Phrasing is implied even though not written: the insistent repeats of bars 12-14 develop into a four-bar phrase (15-18); try imagining from bar 22 onwards as one phrase culminating on the ornament (bar 24) plus an afterthought leading (via an interrupted cadence) into trumpet fanfares at 27; consider a similar shape in bars 30-34 (cadence now perfect, as in equivalent bars 63-64); and two six-note left-hand countermelodies starting from the second beat of bar 36.

Compare bars 34-35 with bars 72-73, one of several inexact repeats that Scarlatti may have forgotten to check (unharmonised 74-75, compared with 34-35, is another). We cannot read

Scarlatti's mind, however, and we should tidy up with caution, if at all, though bar 77's ornament may well match bar 39's – i.e. starting like footnote (1) and comprising eight demis in all – even though notated differently. No argument about the need for clear fingerwork: try right hand 5 2/13 or 4 1/25 over barline 26/27, 15 2-slide-2/1 over barline 52/53 – and if the left hand really can't match previous right-hand ornaments in bars 6 and 8, try cheating and play bars 5-8 with crossed hands: it can't really be wrong to do this if the ornament then sounds better.

Kuhlau	Sonata	
	(no. 2 of *Trois sonates non difficiles* op. 60)	Trinity Guildhall

Anyone with dismissive memories of that Kuhlau C major Sonatine in $\frac{3}{8}$ time for beginners should look again. Although labelled 'non difficile' this A major example is quite spectacular, and – rewardingly – sounds harder than it is, especially at the right tempo. This should be steady enough for full tone in all the scales and broken chords, and for the numerous non-synchronisations between the hands (ends of bars 12, 14, 16 and so on) to sound deliberate rather than just like bad timing. Check the semiquaver upbeats first (like bars 2, 4, 6 and 10), for without left-hand quavers against which to measure them it's tempting to play them too early, like full quavers. Yet quavers are what's required in bars 3, 5, 20 and their equivalents in the recap. (bars 71, 73 and 55). The overall form of this movement is teasing, the second subject (in the mediant minor, unusually) being recapitulated (in tonic minor, from bar 44) before the first subject, which is left until last (bar 69).

As always in music of this period, when the right hand is busy (here, with scales and broken chords), check the exact durations of left-hand notes: almost always crotchets (bars 22, 28, 30 and 59, to take examples at random) but just twice – bars 77 and 78 – minims. This the age (c.1824) of generalised rather than ultra-precisely placed dynamics: the octaves in bars 8 and 10 are of course abrupt, but bar 9's written *p* could be taken a quaver earlier, and bar 3 could shade off towards bar 4's *p*, which in the context is not necessarily *subito*. Similarly, shade off feminine endings even where not marked, as in bars 12, 14 and 35: and if nervous of the quick right-hand leap with which bar 59 starts, try taking its first right-hand semiquaver in the left hand instead. Concerning Kuhlau himself, discoveries are still being made. It was thought – on account of the vast quantity of flute music he composed – that he played the flute himself. This now turns out to be a myth: he merely knew a very good flautist. And anyone who thinks there isn't enough Kuhlau will be sorry to learn that a lot of his manuscripts were destroyed in a house fire in 1832. The smoke from it brought on a chest ailment which caused his death that same year.

Chopin	Mazurka in A minor, op. 67 no. 4	Trinity Guildhall

Among the Polish country people from whose folk music the Mazurka developed, pathos is an admirable quality: a sign of strength, not weakness. This may explain why more than half of Chopin's 51 mazurkas are in the minor mode (there are seven in A minor alone). The name Mazurka actually derives from that of Mazoria, the old name of the province where Chopin grew up. It's a dance, of course, with the accent falling on the third beat just as often as on the first: hence the typical ties and slurs over barlines like 0/1, 8/9, 16/17, 20/21 (a slur not a tie here, so repeat the A) and passionate 28/29. Some places – like bars 2/3, 4/5, 35/36 and 36/37 – work very well if pedalled with this accentuation in mind: pedal down on third beat, up – or changed – on first.

Another characteristic of the Mazurka is that somewhere there will be a faster section, often marked *con anima*. There's no actual marking in this piece, but the place to move on is clearly from bar 33.

Although basically dance music, the tempo may be kept flexible enough to exploit the many soulful moments. Personal choice, these: but if stuck for ideas, then bars 15-16, 28-29, 40/41, 42 (where extra time makes the stretch comfortable), 31-32 (even more so on the reprise, bars 76-80) and before bar 49 (where the unpedalled E may linger) are all good places to experiment – though pausing on the very last note of the piece may sound self-indulgent. Chopin's harmony is always rich and makes rewarding progress: for instance, listen to the left-hand thumb-part in bars 17-32 and try phrasing it as a broken countermelody.

| Tchaikovsky | April (from *The Seasons* op. 37b) | Trinity Guildhall |

Of course April is a month, not a season. Music publisher Nikolai Bernard commissioned twelve pieces from Tchaikovsky for his periodical *La Nouvelliste*, suggesting titles for each movement (this one's was 'Snowdrops'). Composed piecemeal (and entitled *The Months*) from November 1875, they appeared in print one by one, like a serial – but not the whole set. One movement was kept back: the only way subscribers could obtain it (and thus complete the set) was to buy the omnibus volume – to which Bernard then gave the wrong title (*The Seasons*) and a wrong opus number (37, already used for Tchaikovsky's Grand Sonata).

April is an exercise in long *cantabile* melody above – and sometimes within – a gently pulsating accompaniment. The accompaniment is so close to the solo on the keyboard that correct balance is crucial: keep bar 8's alto F's quieter than fading melody note A, and bar 23's 5th-quaver alto A must not sound like a new melody note. Bars 9-11 need slow practice and ultra-careful balance for the theme to emerge: pedalling will help to sustain notes impossible to play finger-*legato*. Non-pedalled quavers elsewhere would sound too dry: try pedalling the first beats of bars 1-4, and both beats of bars 5-8, avoiding smudges by listening carefully. Bar 25 changes mood, becoming more balletic with repetitive two-bar phrases: there are eight chances to get bar 26's left hand correct but practise it alone nevertheless, avoiding collisions between thumbs when you add right hand. Imagine clarinet here (doubled by flute an octave higher), then imagine a three-way conversation from bar 33: high violin and middle-register viola, joined by high (37-38) then low (40) cello. Same again from bar 49, low cello earlier this time (53): violin and viola debate through bars 57-58, possibly slowing to usher in bar 39's recalled opening theme. Let the accompaniment dissolve through bars 77-85 (four chords per bar reducing to two then one), and consider a generous *rallentando* during the last two or four bars: very stylish, even if not officially authorised.

Rameau	Le rappel des oiseaux [with ornaments]	
	(from *Baroque Real Repertoire*)	Trinity Faber

You would expect grace notes in a birdsong piece: this example is full of them, in both hands. If the suggested ♫♫. interpretation (particularly in the left hand) makes the whole piece drag, then switch to ♫♫♪ or even ♫♫ – the last would finish together with (not before) the next semiquaver in the opposite hand, but probably harmlessly. Bar 34's four-hemidemisemiquaver mordent may also be replaced with a single acciaccatura C if necessary, and bar 52's mordent (whatever you do with it) may affect the resumed tempo in 53. Semiquaver left-hand rests in bars 11-13 do not imply syncopated octave slurs but merely keep the left hand out of the right's way, and as far as possible should sound like all-quaver bars 14-16.

During practice, check note-holding, and more particularly note-lifting, from (*legato* but unpedalled) bar 34, pausing on fourth quaver of bar 35. Here the left-hand A should be held, likewise the alto D: treble E may be harmlessly held (it fits the chord) but F♯ should definitely be clear, similarly throughout. Odd-looking bar 43 contains continuous semiquaver movement: here the alto G must be carefully lifted. Dynamics may be partly deduced from the texture: virtuosic demis at bars 22, and particularly against busy semis in bars 33 and 52, imply louder rather than softer dynamics, as do the descending octaves through bars 24-26. Most of the rest may be ***p*** (make bar 28's sudden key change ***p*** *subito*) – these are small songbirds, not vultures.

J S Bach	French Suite no. 6 in E, BWV 817: Allemande	
	(from *French Suites*)	Bärenreiter *or* Peters

A gentle prelude to the whole suite (and followed there by a brisker Courante), this need not exceed ♩ = 92. Many alternative fingerings are possible: in choosing your own, don't neglect the possibility of fingering black notes with thumb (e.g. right hand 1525 1214 to start bar 4; 5 2123 5142 or 4 1212 4142 to end bar 18). More important is consistency of phrasing: right-hand semiquavers may all be *legato* but left hand may start ♫♫♫♫♫ or ♫♫♫♫♫♪. Whatever you choose, treat bars 5-8 and 13-14 the same way. Breathe in the right-hand part too, say before both F♯s in bar 8, before paired semiquavers and offbeat crotchets thereafter (simile, in either hand, from 16/17 to 23). Expressive left hand may slur the first four notes over barlines 14/15 and (softer) 15/16 while octave leaps before rests may be *staccato*.

Ornaments may be simplified, especially in bars 8 (the mordent is important, the turn possibly less so) and 11 (where the mordent may be reduced to a single grace note before the beat). Dynamics – try ***mf*** at start and bars 4, 14/15 and 19; ***f*** at 8, 11 (halfway through), 12/13, 24 (halfway through) and 27; ***mp*** at 5, 6, 8 (halfway through), 18, 21 (halfway through) and 26; ***p*** at 5 (halfway through), 6 (halfway through), 16/17, 20 (halfway through) and 25 – and *cresc.* from 2, 7, 9 (halfway through), 22 (halfway through) and 27.

Haydn **Sonata in B minor, Hob XVI/32, 1st movement: Allegro moderato**
(from *Sonatas* vol. IV *or Selected Sonatas* vol. 1) **Peters *or* Henle**

Forget the image of Haydn as a lightweight substitute for students not yet ready for Beethoven. This B minor Sonata movement is brooding, almost sullen, propelled by a leaden bass line in *pesante* quavers. Tempo is a quick eight in the bar (*c.♪* = 126-160), respecting the *moderato* part of the instruction and also allowing time for the numerous ornaments.

Ornaments vary between editions, and Haydn was probably not fussy. Some turns in the Peters edition are replaced in other sources by inverted mordents, or even omitted altogether. Small notes in bars 34-35 may equally be on-the-beat semiquaver appoggiaturas or crushed before-the-beat acciaccaturas. Choose according to technique and common sense, matching bars 9-10, 29-30, 31-32, 38 and 48-49 with bars 1-2, for instance, and playing bars 3-4 like Peters or – simpler and equally effective – as follows:

Crotchet-quaver slurs in bars 5-6 should instinctively feel 'strong-weak' (as should the final quavers of bar 12), but bar 7's may *cresc.* continually. The mood lightens from bar 13, where the left-hand chords may be quickly spread for emphasis, while the right hand brings out a theme in duet with tenor from among the semiquavers: this becomes a treble–bass crotchet duet in 17-18. Try one-bar *crescs/dims* in bars 19-20, *cresc.* through bar 21 towards brilliant triplets from 22. End the exposition *senza dim.* with spread chords in both hands, launching melodramatically into the development and rising to ***ff*** on top C (bar 30). Practise bars 43-47 with each slur compressed into three-note chords, noticing non-unison between the hands from 44. Haydn's recapitulations often play tricks, compressing, rearranging or simply omitting chunks of the exposition, but not here, where his main surprise is the replacing of bars 6-12 with just two (53-54). The texture changes from bar 63, and bar 66's dramatic diminished 7th arpeggio may be pedalled. Bar 67 is also an octave higher than you might expect.

Heller **Epilogue (no. 25 from *Melodious Studies* op. 45)** **Alfred**

Here's a surprise if you thought Heller just wrote easy little pieces for beginners. Stephen Heller (1813-1888) and Schumann were mutual admirers even though they never actually met, and this *Epilogue* is as fierce as anything Schumann ever wrote. It's a study in stamina, with fast repeated chords and octaves almost relentless and requiring strong but utterly relaxed wrists and forearms. It is tempting to blur with pedal, but infinitely more effective without: even the printed pedallings in bars 1-3 (if you have them) may be shortened to quaver dabs purely to colour the accents.

Chords in bars 13-15 and 25-43 are also hard to find speedily: practise each group in an altered rhythm of two semiquavers and quaver at first to gain more time. There is no shame in giving the arm a rest and taking the simpler *ossia* from bar 33, ready for the renewed onslaught (originally *f*, now ***ff***) from bar 44. Bar 59 should probably have ***sf*** to match bar 63, but the non-***sf***s in bars 64 and 66 are correct. Bars 75-78 sound like a recitative, but instead of the expected cadential G7/C on a harpsichord we get a long self-quote from Study no. 1, *The Brook*, which students and teachers may already know. The right hand, with crotchet melody waiting to be picked out of the semiquavers, resembles Debussy's *Dr Gradus ad Parnassum* (see Grade 8) while the left hand tests accurate note holding. Check A and C♯s through bars 91 and 93; memorise the falling two-note crotchet pattern in 96-97, and resume Tempo I (possibly not printed) at 98 even if only for three bars. 102's tremolo is heavy and not too fast: crotchet pedals may clarify the descending right hand better than one long one, though bar 104's bass octave C should be pedalled and the final chord added to it without changing.

Chabrier	Feuillet d'album	
	(from *Complete Works for Piano or* separately)	Dover *or* Enoch

This 'Albumleaf' is surprisingly melancholy if all you know of Chabrier is *España*. Its eventual key (A major) is teasingly delayed, much of the opening sounding closer to F♯ minor and only fleetingly touching home base (root-position A major in bar 8) *en route* to the reassuring V-I cadence at 15/16. A slow waltz, it may remind you of Debussy's *La plus que lente*, and its theme in parallel octaves with juicy harmonies (from 17/18) or two octaves apart (from 40/41) may recall Ravel – who incidentally wrote a homage piece 'in the style of Chabrier'.

This tests the ability to balance tune and accompaniment, the inner parts of bars 1-5 obviously being far quieter than the theme which must itself be gentle. Practise just the theme, unaccompanied, developing a melodic shape you like (*cresc.*, *rubato*, etc.), then aim for the same with accompaniment restored. Notice many *crescendo*s followed by (*subito*) ***p*** or ***pp***, e.g. bars 8-9, 14-15, 23-24. Check easily misread augmented seconds in 18 and 22; finger the left hand of (pedalled) bars 25-26 with thumb on third note, then 27 with 53 214 321. Balance is crucial from 32/33, ***pp*** violins being accompanied by gentle (***pppp***) harp in the next room. Finger bar 46 (right hand) with repeated 124 – and don't repedal the ***ppp*** chords in 47-48, or you'll lose the bass.

Fauré	Romance sans paroles op. 17 no. 3	
	(from *Romantic Real Repertoire*)	Trinity Faber

This, the most popular of the three op. 17 pieces that Fauré wrote around 1863, may remind you of the even better-known Berceuse from the *Dolly Suite*: the accompanying rhythm is the same, and the main tune similarly returns in canon. On just two hands rather than the Berceuse's four, the canon here (bars 41-53) requires many split-second right-hand leaps, which are tricky to accomplish without bumps that would damage the fabric of Fauré's naturally fragile sound-world.

As with his third Impromptu op. 34 in the same key, Fauré's opening pattern may be shared between the hands (here with right hand taking top C, D♭ and E♭) for a smooth start, and rather than just marking time may swell to the third bar and then fade to admit the tune. Whole-bar pedals may continue beyond the introduction: if the slight treble smearing is less acceptable to you than losing the implied minim bass-line, revert to the suggested crotchet pedals. Bar 11's triplet must not slip into semiquaver-quaver-semiquaver; passionate bar 18's *con suono* (literally, 'with sound') means sonorously. 'Strong-weak' phrasing is compulsory in bars 31-32 and 39-40, where the right hand may take top left-hand note to avoid bumping. Bars 61-62 and 65-66 contain a distant descant; try catching bars 68-72's grace notes with pedal, and adding *una corda* to achieve the ***ppp*** from bar 71.

Group B

Martinů   The Shy Puppet (Chanson) (no. 3 of *Puppets*, book 1)   Trinity Guildhall

Martinů was born Czech, but spent much time in Paris, and you may feel some Gallic insouciance applies to the numbering of his three books of Puppets: Book 3 was composed in 1912, Book 2 in 1918 and this Book 1 in 1924! The Shy Puppet is well-named, staying hesitant and rather self-effacing: the odd $\frac{2}{4}$ bar adds unexpected charm to the first four-bar phrase. Bars 12-17 gain confidence, though staying light rather than thrusting even at the *f* of bar 28, and shouting only once, in bars 35-36. Notice the subtitle *Chanson*: secure maximum singing *legato* in *pp* bars 18-19 by fingering right hand with 124 135 124 135–slide–135 124 123 124. Compare the different articulations of bars 1-3 and 18-20 (20 being even shyer, with slighter *crescs* and no *tenuto* marks), and confirm B♮ against B♭ in third beat of bar 15. Count strictly from bar 37, with no *ritard.* until marked, and no more than a bar's silence before the D.C.. Bar 16's printed fingering makes the upper voice perfectly *legato* but if uncomfortable (third chord contains C♯, notice) try 135 24 35 13 24 13 53; anyone uncomfortable with the same-note finger changing in the right hand from bar 24 may try – for instance – 525/4321 over bar-line 24/25. If you enjoy playing music in this style, try the same composer's *Etudes* and *Polkas*.

Quilter   Shepherd Song (no. 1 of *Country Pieces* op. 27)   Trinity Guildhall

Anyone comparing the ebullient music of Percy Grainger with this reflective *Shepherd Song* (composed in 1923) may be surprised to learn that the two composers were once in the same group, named 'The Frankfurt Gang' (its members having studied there together). The other members were Cyril Scott (he of *Lotus Land*), Balfour Gardiner (ditto *Shepherd's Fennel Dance*) and Norman O'Neill (sadly, composer of nothing famous at all). Like Schubert, Roger Quilter always had the sound of the voice in mind even when writing instrumentally, and every bar here sounds like a song transcription.

The very steady metronome mark is a reminder to think two-in-a-bar rather than plod in six, yet gives plenty of time to pedal individual quavers. Be generous with pedal (specifically marked places – like bars 8 and 16 – do not preclude pedal elsewhere) particularly anywhere awkward to finger-*legato* easily, for nothing here should sound effortful. Take care not to double the speed by mistake at bar 17's crotchets, and notice that the alto here becomes roughly inverted four bars later on; the main theme reappears differently harmonised from bar 34. Convey breathless excitement from bar 25 with carefully observed rests in the 'voice' part over alternately held and lifted 5th-finger bass notes – and double-check L/R synchronisation in broken rhythms, both here and in bars 38-39 (memorise the meaning of *slentando* by noticing the word *lento* hidden in it). The reprise (from bar 39/40) compresses 16 bars into 8, and is tricky to memorise: bar 41 is more like bar 14 than bar 2, bars 45-46's dynamics more like bars 14-15 than 7-8, and the melodic turn over barline 46-47 is quite new. Read slurs and ties carefully: B's, G♯s and C♯s repeat in bars 49-50, as the articulation marks (mostly) tell you. Resist the temptation to repedal on the penultimate chord: you are carefully asked not to.

| Hancock-Child | Leo (from *Zodiac – 12 Preludes*) | Trinity Guildhall |

If you like the sound of relaxed big band swing, thank composer and piano accompanist Rosemary Hancock-Child for this chance to play some. All Leos, on this evidence are wonderful people: outgoing, generous, warm-hearted and the most modest folk you could ever hope to meet. Once past the bass lion's-roars of the first four bars, this piece proceeds with a big smile and a large drink. The juiciness of the chords depends on careful reading, with deliberate clashes between the hands like the G natural against flat in bar 1 and against sharp in bar 2. Conversely, the non-clash in bar 19 (C♯ 'against' D♭) is there purely for grammatical reasons, with two voices moving in opposite harmonic directions. Make the theme more prominent than the accompaniment, however interesting the latter may be: keep bars 8 and 18's chords quiet, ditto bar 37's left hand run-up and bar 41's fill-in triplet figure. Less obviously, consider bars 14 and 16's high treble passages as a quiet afterthought even though under the same phrase mark: conversely, continue an unbroken theme right through bar 43 (pause included) to 44. Phrase marks ending in mid-air, as it were, rather than directly on a note (like bars 8, 18 and 41) hint that the melody flows unbroken into the next phrase. Bar 32 is a variation of bar 7, hence the odd-looking six-quaver triplet: phrase this, subtly, as three pairs, copying alto in bar 34. Bar 35's fourth-beat chord is an accompaniment, not a solo (matching equivalent bar 10); finger-hold the last three bars even though pedalling, and release the pedal punctually to reveal the plain C major triad (like a wink) on which to close.

| Johnston | Grumpy Trolls | Trinity Guildhall |

Look beyond the child-friendly title, jokey tempo marking (*Presto Groucho*) and deliberately wrong crashing last note: this is a frenetic gallop through a dark and sinister forest that may remind you of Liszt – or even the Lord of the Rings. Its near-nonstop right hand triplets require untiring energy, and controlled co-ordination to stop them tumbling out of order at speed – the 'high-low–middle-note' sequence can so easily slip into 'high-middle-low' in the general excitement. Read carefully: there are almost no cautionary accidentals in this piece: no A♭s in bar 11 after bar 10's A♮s, for instance, nor G♮s in bar 95 after bar 94's G♯s.

Try practising the entire right hand with each quaver group compressed into a three-note chord to learn the hand shapes securely: you then have to negotiate some awkward right-hand corners (over barlines 13/14 and 21/22, which you could also try fingering 524/31) and fast moves from one pattern to the next, as in bars 61-64. If struggling here, turn it to advantage by starting steadier (and heavier, as if hauling yourself back up to speed) after bar 56's *rit*. Most of the fun (with melody notes picked out *en route*) lies in the right hand, but the left hand has its own drama, not only in those plunging bass notes (in bars like 9-16) but, more subtly, in the changes from detached crotchets to full-length dotted crotchets which are worth phrasing as solid countermelodies. Bar 73 explodes in a cloud of dust, twigs and squawking birds as the whole earth splits open underfoot. Bars 81-86 are still *ff*, and clangorous: bar 86 is *p* subito, and the printed *subito **mp*** at bar 91 tells you that the *cresc.* just beforehand should be *molto*. Switch to the closing duplets without flagging, and hit the last note deliberately, and very hard indeed.

Janáček	Come with Us!, from *On an Overgrown Path* (from *Twentieth Century Real Repertoire*)	Trinity Faber

Janáček was a passionate patriot and country lover, prone to violent changes of mood; his vivid and original music sometimes needed unconventional notation. Here, the ⅛ bars and septuplets (one against a triplet, in the same hand!) are less daunting to play than they look, and you will be enchanted by the folksy six-note falling phrase that first appears in bar 3 and pervades the rest of the piece.

Treat the first ⅛ bar as a simple upbeat, and treat combined bars 13-14 as a simple ⅝ bar. To deal with the septuplets, take bar 23's *rit.* a fraction earlier than printed, and play as if the first six chords were a 2/4 bar of quaver triplets, then adding one more chord in the same pulse. Think bar 24 either in a slower 2/4, placing the second, third and fourth alto notes further and further ahead of the treble, finishing the bar slightly out of time (as in example 1 below) – alternatively, count this bar in ⅞ (and play as example 2). Both examples are mathematically inexact, but only by a few milliseconds.

Example 1   Example 2

Mainly innocent, this volatile music is suddenly neurotic at bars 10-11: its *accel.* may be repeated at similar bars 29-30 even though not printed there. The two-bar increases in volume from bar 19 are effective and traditional though not in the original: the **ppp** at bar 25 is an authentic Janáček stroke of genius. The opening repeat must be made, and the very end (bar 32) must be deliberately abrupt, with no hint of a pause.

Poulenc	Nocturne no. 8 (from *Nocturnes*)	Heugel

Francis Poulenc constantly changed musical styles, often within a few bars. This Nocturne, however, is consistently gentle and melodious, like Schubert with a few updated chords. The French instruction means 'Use pedal a lot (the melody brought out gently and the pulsations [*the repeated chords*] very unobtrusive).' The melody starts in octaves, not just single notes, and is partly recalled – a beat out – from bar 12. Breathe without losing the pulse at each phrase ending; take a little longer (say an added semiquaver rest, no more) at the four printed commas. Try *rubato*, pushing on in bars 5 and 21, more so in bars 17-18, calming down in proportion during bars 8, 12, 19 and particularly 27 ('very relaxed'), rippling and crossing hands without harassment.

Ending in C not G seems odd: this eighth Nocturne closes a cycle that began in that key, however, and the ending is a direct quote from no. 1. Other odd sounds may be accidental: check F#s in bars 10-11 (amid all those flats) and 29, E♮ in 19, A♭ through bar 21 and E♭ plus F# through bar 23. French ties (those leading to nothing, as it were) in bars 33-34 imply one long pedal.

Kabalevsky	Sonatina op. 13 no. 1, 3rd movement: Presto	
	(from *Sonatinas for piano* op. 13 nos. 1 & 2)	Boosey & Hawkes

Dmitri Kabalevsky's two op. 13 Sonatinas exist in two editions: the 1933 original was the only one available until 1994, despite being revised in 1969. The revised works are available in one album: differences in Sonata no. 2 are fundamental, but those in this C major work are tiny: some fingerings are changed, the same-pulse relationship of bars 42-43 is confirmed, and some short pedals are added to bars 2 and 3. This controlled gallop of a movement remains popular with young pianists, being long enough to form a recital piece and sounding harder to play than it actually is.

Tenuto lines over single notes indicate slight accents, as on the first eight downbeats where they clarify the $\frac{9}{8}$ time signature to listeners. They are gentler than 'real' accents – check through bars 15-18 and 70-72 – while unaccented notes, like the left-hand chords through bars 19-26, may be kept light. (Sustain right hand over *staccato* left hand, particularly in bars 21-22 and 25-26.) The thinned-out triad in bar 31 is to make room for the right hand. Bar 47, of course, occupies both hands, melodic minor scale in the right and minor arpeggio in the left. Compare *f* here with *pp* four bars later. The last notes of bars 57 and 60 are not chromatic, notice; the left hand in bar 58 has A♮ (not ♭), to match 55. Practise 70-72 two octaves apart, or crossed hands, to hear the left hand better and check that it is as good as the right. The recapitulation starts at bar 73: mouth-organ harmonies at 81-84 now add *crescs/dims* (equivalent bars 9-12 did not), while second subject (bar 92, triumphantly in major mode) is now *f*, originally (bar 19) *p*. Finish boldly, *poco allargando* in bar 131 with positively no *dim*.

P, S & O	Wedgwood Blue [Theme and *either* Variation 1 *or* Variation 2]	
Wedgwood	(from *Wedgwood Blue*)	Faber

Pam Wedgwood is famous for *Jazzin' About* and similar pieces for students at all stages. *Wedgwood Blue* is a family affair, Pam herself supplying a gently swinging theme and sons Sam and Olly one variation each. The suggested metronome mark is relaxed indeed, a cowboy 'old-timer' snoozing on his verandah in the sun, momentarily serious in bars 15-18 (straight quavers here), elsewhere thoroughly at ease, with grace notes gently smeared onto the main notes and minim pedals joining each bass note to avoid dryness. Check the odd enharmonics – barline 7/8 should sound like $B^7/E+^7$ – and add a left-hand pause (matching the right) before the very last bass 'button'.

Sam's variation is barely faster than the theme, lingering over juicy moments like barline 3/4 and bar 5, with a comma maybe before bar 8. The 'big band' section (from 16/17) should be noticeably livelier, and may copy the punchy sounds of close-harmony brass and (from 26, itself launching a variation of the previous eight bars) walking string bass; the close (bars 36-44) should have a 'work-song' feel, soloist answered by choral 'Oh yeah!'.

Olly's variation is funky, and all quavers are straight, not swung. Higher chords in bars 1-4 may take biting accents, even if subdued in the general *p* dynamic. Bar 12's chord ripples downwards; notice the long build-up from mysterious opening to full brass outburst at 21-23. Bar 32's *8va* chord is a far-distant ripple amid the free but still rhythmic E♭ minor section. Bars 47-50 are a long fade-out: try playing the printed theme, first time only, then improvise. For how long? The companion CD goes round six times, using notes from the indicated scale but ranging up a couple of octaves more.

Grade 8

Group A

J S Bach	Prelude from English Suite no. 3 BWV 808	Trinity Guildhall

Bach's six English Suites were designed on a grander scale than the French Suites (see Grade 5), and this magnificent opening movement will sound suitably dramatic in performance if imagined as the first movement of a harpsichord concerto with string orchestra (or even a concerto with three soloists, for the 'Solo' passages are laid out in three parts rather than two, adding great richness to the sound). Orchestrating it thus, even if only mentally, can provide many suggestions for effective dynamics. Here's how it might go: full orchestra (string parts entering one by one) through to bar 33 − *f* at the start, possibly *mf* from bar 16, then *f* from 24. Solo enters (*p*) at 33, violins making discreet references to the opening (*mp*, maybe) in bars 43–45 and 53–55; *f* (orchestra) again from bar 67, *mf* at 82 if that's how 16 went ('same music, same level' makes the overall structure clear); new solo at 99, orchestra entering voice by voice from 107, and so on. The only new material thereafter is the extra drama Bach cunningly weaves into the final solo (from bar 161), with trills and diminished-seventh harmonies like those in the first movement of Brandenburg Concerto no. 5.

Technically, release all notes except the held ones in bars like 17–20, where it's fatally easy to glue everything down in an overall *tenuto*; similarly, carefully hold or repeat in the right hand exactly as bars 90–98 specify, and notice the moving middle part in the right hand over barline 97/98. Practise the left hand alone over barlines 45 and 55 (the printed 5th finger is vital for reaching the middle part). Avoid runaway left-hand semis from bar 162 as the right hand trills: write out the footnote (4) on the stave itself if necessary, to double-check the actual synchronisation between the hands, noticing that every left-hand note coincides with the upper trill note, not the lower. Slur (and shade off) the appoggiaturas and their resolutions in bars like 25 and 27. Left-hand chords in bars 7, 115 and 187 may be quickly arpeggiated for Baroque-style emphasis. Tempo − remember that semiquavers in Bach are generally melodic, while demisemis (bars 35, 43 and so on) are bravura flourishes.

Beethoven	Sonata in C, op. 2 no. 3, 3rd movement: Scherzo & Trio	Trinity Guildhall

This is the grandest of the three op. 2 sonatas dedicated to Haydn, who may well have been startled by some features while undoubtedly enjoying the humour and dramatic contrasts of this Scherzo. Tempo is crucial: it's tempting to take the Scherzo at a gallop, but the arpeggio-feature Trio should really go no slower. Keep steady, making time to phrase the three quavers as ordinary quavers (i.e. not triplets) with no bump on the first quaver. A steady tempo is also helpful in those treacherous 'land gently' leaps from bar 29. Whether in *cantabile* dotted minims or *staccato* crotchets (marked or unmarked − Beethoven's manuscript was a little casual, e.g. at bar 7, where left hand is marked *staccato* but right hand not), this music proceeds not in one-bar but four-bar phrases, and should be shaped accordingly. The one exception, the unaccompanied three-bar phrase in bars 36–38, heralds the return of the scherzo theme, and could conceivably take a *poco rit*. Old editions added a *p* halfway through bar 39, to avoid bar 41's alto apparently coming in louder than the treble it imitates. This *p* is not in the manuscript, but could discreetly be reinstated in performance.

No need for more unwritten dynamics in the Scherzo (any *crescendos* are ready-built into the texture, like the octaves in bars 23-27) – but the Trio cannot plausibly start at the last printed dynamic (***ff***), so it may start ***f***, ***mf*** or even ***p***. The strong little-finger top notes are sometimes (but not always) accented, as from bars 73-74: in between times (bars like 75-76) – after checking right-hand thumb notes to ensure correct harmony – try going *meno* ***f***, while picking out and shaping a little-finger melody (a longer one in similar bars 86-88), then *decresc.* in bar 76 so that 77 has something to *cresc.* from. Try eccentric-looking fingering 1/2451 over barline 80/81 to avoid a potentially difficult thumb hop. Arpeggios in bars 102-103 are written to be played all in the right hand, but if nervous try going hand over hand, taking the third group F/D-B-G (the one over the barline) with the left hand. (Last three notes of all are obviously in left hand.) Count rests in strict time when making the *D.C.*, and when entering the *Coda*, where the left-hand accents in bars 111-112 obviously continue to the end.

Mendelssohn	Song without Words op. 67 no. 2	Trinity Guildhall

Purely technically, this is a rapid study in light *staccato* (mostly unpedalled), plus a sustained *cantabile* melody. Even at this basic level it is a challenging option, requiring skilful holding of single fingers while background *staccatos* proceed beneath, above and sometimes around them.

$\frac{12}{16}$ time equals four counts per bar, of course, each beat equalling one dotted quaver: the piece therefore starts halfway through a bar. The left hand is technically a little awkward right at the start: if nervous, try alternative fingering 514213/ (or even 5-hop-21312/), and 513231/ a bar later. The right-hand thumb often has to hop between semiquavers: do this without bumping and persevere in places like bars 5, 6 and 7, where the reiterated notes are actually easier to articulate with a thumb. Some right-hand melody notes are tricky to finger-hold, or to play *legato*: try closing bar 6 with 4-slide-4 (G#-A), giving 5 time to prepare for the next C#. Change finger exactly where printed in bar 15, for 3 must hold while later notes lift. If bar 49's printed 3-4 is awkward, sustain the A instead with split-second pedal (after *staccatos* have finished), similarly in the following bars. *Staccato* and *legato* occasionally coincide, as on the second beat of bars 29 and 33: here, play (don't tie) the semiquaver B, then sustain it as part of the upper voices, similarly on second beat of bar 38 where R and L collide. Bar 48's grace notes should be tucked in as quickly as possible, to maintain the overall momentum.

To understand this piece musically, play the whole piece through with just the tune (fingered how you like) and bass, but with no middle-register semis. Include both *legato* voices (helpfully marked 'a2') from bars 28-44 as you do this. This 'simplified version' will disclose highly suitable breath marks, e.g. after two notes in bars 8, 10-12, 20, 24, 26,28, 35-36, 38 and 42. Incorporate these, plus other subtle shaping you discover *en route* (notice some unpredictable dynamics), when you then reinstate the middle-register semis. They will swamp the top note in bars 15-16 because of the requested *cresc.* to ***f***, but this doesn't matter. Gently bring out the top notes of the final two chords, to highlight the difference between them.

C Schumann — Witches' Dance
(no. 1 of *Quatre pièces charactéristiques* op. 5) — Trinity Guildhall

This energetic piece may seem repetitive, and its dynamic and articulation marks not closely thought through. Be tolerant: Clara Schumann (or Wieck as she was then) was only 15 or 16 when she composed it. The *Witches' Dance* is sustained by a few technical devices, making it a good study (in both hands equally, be warned) for leaps, double thirds and grace notes. Read carefully: most grace notes are a semitone below the main note, but some are a whole tone above. In any event, and however fast you eventually go, carefully articulate them before (not crushed together with) the main note. It's safe to resume the prevailing dynamic (often *p*) after each *sf* – and enjoy the cross-rhythm these markings produce in bars 41-44 and 71-74. They disappear for a while after bar 96 – possibly through oversight but the reading is valid without them: bar 97 could well be basically *pp*, hushed before the *f* of bars 101-10. The newly placed downbeat *sf*s in bars 107 and 111 (against repeated *p* nearby) may mean 'these two bars stay *f*'. Harmonies are straightforward and predictable, though remember unsignalled G♮s in bar 8 after earlier G♯s. The chromatic scale with grace notes in bars 15-16 – and particularly 74-80 – is fun to play once learned, but observe that the last two main notes are diatonic, breaking the pattern. Quavers without dots may probably be played *staccato*: carefully written demisemi rests in bars like 3-4 may imply no pedal there; short marked pedals elsewhere do not preclude similar use elsewhere, though be sparing. Pedal may provide covering fire as you leap dizzily from one register to another, but the risk of blurring lies permanently in wait.

J S Bach — Prelude and Fugue in F minor, BWV 881
(from *The Well-tempered Clavier* book 2) — Bärenreiter *or* Peters

This Prelude and Fugue is one of the most joyously singable pairs of works from Book 2 of the '48'; the Prelude's alternate mimicking of two voices and lute figuration is most attractive, as is the bouncy episode theme in the Fugue.

Many editions suggest mordents to start the Prelude's first two bars. If repeated systematically, they can sound fussy, and no real harm comes from leaving them out: the expressive 'lift/lean-lift' phrasing is far more important. (Mordents in bars 40-46 are obligatory, however – in this context they may go on or even before the beat.) The 'lute' (think 'guitar') figuration (bars 4/5-8, etc.) may even be discreetly pedalled on each left-hand quaver. Notice that bars 20/21-24 vary the opening theme and place it in the left hand, accompanying with harmonies best appreciated by compression into four-note crotchet chords during practice. 20/21-26 are notated as tenor-bass duet while smoother equivalent bars 63-68 (now with ties, not rests) eventually coalesce into one voice – an intriguing variation. Most editions show a chromatically descending alternative left hand in bar 50 (which many players prefer) to emphasise the resemblance to the opening theme: but hardly any version suggests quickly arpeggiating bar 69's dramatic diminished 7th chords, let alone pausing on the second of them, but this is a highly valid interpretation. Speed: try ♩ = 76-84.

As always, the fugue subject needs consistent phrasing on each appearance: try

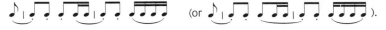

As in the Prelude, the mordent is optional and might cause problems if you tried to fit it into the middle voice (bars 29, 51 and 75). Dropping to *p* for the subject tail (halfway through bar 2-bar 4) could weaken the piece; save *p* for the singalong episode theme in bars 17-24, 33-40 (*cresc.* here) and 66-71 (but not bars 78-85, best done *f*). Whenever this recurs with the voices reallocated (bars 33-35, 66-68) the fourth quaver should be replayed then tied over the barline to clarify the unison writing. Occasionally play each voice separately, right through from bar 1 to 85, noticing real fugal entries and enjoying the bass's false ones (bars 56-68, 62-64) and virtuoso cello part in 78-85. Each part is singable almost all the way through, except for syncopated hiccups like bar 40's alto and 56-57's treble. These are mere instructions to sustain for full value.
Speed: ♩ = anything between 69 and 92.

Haydn	Sonata in B♭, Hob. XVI: 41, 1st movement: Allegro
	(from *Piano Sonatas Selection* vol. 2) Henle *or* Wiener Urtext

With several Haydn sonatas in the same key, and without the standardised numbering of, say, Beethoven's sonatas, double-check that you have the right piece. It's no. 55 in the Wiener Urtext, no. 27 in Peters' vol. 3, while the old Augener/Franklin Taylor edition numbered it 19. It starts with a chord and dotted-rhythm descending scale of B♭ major, and an F minor theme with left-hand triplets follows in bar 25. This basically joyous piece has just a few darker moments, and a comically abrupt key change at bar 56.

A tempo of ♩ = 66-76 will add sparkle to the semiquaver runs yet leave just enough time to preserve snappy demisemis in bars like 2 and 40 (easily – and wrongly – slackened into semis) and to articulate those grace notes amid semiquavers in bars 8, 10 and 12. The triplet sections (typically, from bar 25) demand thought, for they accompany themes in what look on paper like mismatching rhythms. These can sound stilted if played strictly as written, and in performance the right-hand quavers of bars 25 and 27, and paired semiquavers of bars 26 and 28, could synchronise with (rather than precede) the third note of the triplet. Trills and other nearby ornaments, if written out, would look more fearsome on the page than they are in performance: the fourth beat of bar 25 may be played as a quintuplet filling a crotchet (as may the one in bar 68, even though notated differently), while the trills in bars 26 and 35-39 fit easily against the left hand if played as semiquaver sextuplets.

Appoggiaturas in bars 29 and 30, if not already transcribed in your edition, should be played as two crotchets: Haydn wrote mordents in bars 32-34 and trills in the equivalent recapitulation bars 128-130, but almost certainly intended every one to sound the same. This is not the only casually-notated place: many left-hand chords (bars 1, 13, 21-22, 60, 94 and 142-143, for instance) may be quickly arpeggiated even though not marked. Printed dynamics are sparse (non-existent at the beginning: try starting *f*, dropping to *p* in bar 9) and cannot possibly imply, for instance, unrelieved *f* through bars 24-49. Deduce a scheme from the harmonic flow and texture changes, dropping (say) to *meno f* at 27, *p* at 29, *cresc.* at 33, *f* at 35, and *p cresc.* to *f* through the 'Ready? Sure? Get set! Go!' chromatic-scale sequence from bars 43-47 (abridged in equivalent bars 138-141 by omitting the 'Sure?' half-bar), and tweaking the printed dynamics so that bars 52-55 have the same shape as 48-51. More subtly, think in long *cantabile* phrases that in effect absorb any short-slur articulation marks, making two-bar phrases in bars 9-12 and 25-37, for instance, and a *cantabile* left hand countermelody in bars 14 and 16. Haydn had a childlike (not childish) sense of humour, and the mad key change at bar 56 sounds even funnier when the second half is repeated: no time for this in the exam, of course, but a joke to savour in concert performance.

| Mozart | Sonata in D, K. 284, 1st movement: Allegro |
| | (from *Piano Sonatas* vol. I) | Henle *or* Wiener Urtext |

This piece is extrovert and breezy, though never aggressive like Beethoven. It needs well-controlled semiquavers in either hand, some hand-crossing, long trills over semis, some *cantabile* right-hand octaves, acute rhythm to distinguish demisemis from semis (and to articulate the former cleanly) – and more subtle skills like the picking out of melodies buried in semis (e.g. left hand in bars 17-20, right hand in 30-32) plus an instinct for Mozartian phrasing like the slight 'strong-weak' slurs above sustained alto in bars 34-36 and the over-the-barline phrasing for crossed-over left hand in bars 53-60.

At ♩ = 132 the demisemis in thirds at bars 40 and 43 may be troublesome to articulate, but a slower overall tempo may drag. End bar 1 with eight equal semiquavers if your edition does not already translate the appoggiaturas like this. Bars 1-4 comprise one *f* phrase but printed *p*/*f*s at bars 4/5-7 may go *p* cresc./*mf* dim., with *cresc.* in bar 8 to regain a real *f* at 9. Start bar 10's demis after, not with, second bass note; compare similar bars 40 and 43, and imagine repeated quavers through 44 to preserve exact rhythm there. Bar 22 switches from swagger to calm though without losing speed; maintain power (weak fingers notwithstanding) through the ends of bars 30-32. Pedal four crotchets in bar 48 and a whole bar in 49 (where the left hand must not lose time), for richness of tone – not to hide imperfections in the trill!

Check harmony changes in bars 62 (C♯ before ♮) and similarly 64 (B♮ before ♭); then easily-missed C♯s through bars 66-67. The recapitulation contains, rarely for Mozart (though to become common in Beethoven), a passage seeming to want notes above the available range of the piano: bars 109 and 124 have to alter the right hand of equivalent bars 37 and 48 simply in order to fit. Mozart's alteration is skilfully managed, and editorial alternatives going beyond top F are not compulsory. Other changes affect bars 105 (right hand) and 106 (left hand) – compare with bars 33-34 – bars 121-123 (compare 45-47) and include an extra bar (97) of showing-off.

Mendelssohn	Scherzo in E minor, op. 16 no. 2
	(from *Selected Songs Without Words and Scherzo in E minor*
	or Piano Works vol. II)	Kjos *or* Peters

In a more innocent age, this could have been dubbed 'fairy music' – it inhabits the same delicate, miniaturised world as the *Midsummer Night's Dream* overture and would make an ideal preparation for the more ambitious *Andante and Rondo Capriccioso*. A light touch is paramount; loose wrists are also vital, at *pp* and *ff*. Take the tempo from the tricky repeated chords of bars 3-4, 41/42-45 and 53/54-56. The few *f*s are abrupt, and *crescendo*s rare: *pp* staccato phrases should nevertheless be shaped, grace notes indicating the (tiny) climaxes in bars 4/5-8 and the toytown merry-go-round episode at 21-24. Trumpet- and horn-calls at 16/17 and 30/31 (lift bass, hold tenor, same at 34) are reminders from the full-size world, but fail to disrupt the atmosphere until 39/40. Memorise double octaves at bars 58-61 (*cresc.* as you descend) and in performance watch where your thumbs land. Left hand leads, right hand follows, from bar 88 (*p*), catching up at 91 (*pp*); adjust tempo in 96-98 if you've been rushing, for the *Coda* (from 99) must not sound slower. The printed long pedal (10 bars with no change!) is presumably authentic but risks muddying the texture as the fairies disperse: play as lightly as possible.

Liszt	Au lac de Wallenstadt (from *Années de pèlerinage I, Suisse*)	Henle

This is Liszt in dreamy rather than virtuosic mood, needing an instinct for unmarked *rubato* and continuous pedal — though the enormous hand apparently expected from bar 1's printed fingering (Liszt's own) is not vitally necessary. Semiquaver ripples (including bars 1 and 3) may all be fingered 121 3 5 3 2 or 231 2 5 2 1 (excluding those bars which may be shared between the hands so that the unoccupied right hand takes the triplet). Either of these fingerings works well throughout, even in close-position bars like 45–51.

Printed short slurs are like violin bowings, with no real breaks in between: bars 4/5–19 may be treated as two 8-bar phrases or even one 16-bar. Its immediate repeat in octaves will automatically be *sempre dolce* if kept **pp** *senza cresc*. Mark bar 39 very gently, and linger over the punning harmonic switch in bar 43. Bar 52's small rather than large notes imply demisemiquavers in free rather than strict time: slow down progressively from this bar in order to manage octave grace notes without hurrying — just sound each one after (not with) the left hand's final semiquaver. The last two right-hand notes of bars 63–64 and 71–72 will of course synchronise with the left, but strict three-against-two practice of their first beats is almost counterproductive: the theme should simply sound as if gently floating out of phase. The wide skips in 73–74 are *sempre cantabile* rather than a trailer for *La Campanella*, and the right-hand two-octave leaps in 99–102 stay unhurried, with lower note on the beat and gentle upper note any time before the second beat. Bar 80 is easier than it looks (D♮ and F♭ are both played with the thumb) and ♪ = ♪ into bar 103, the $\frac{2}{4}$ time signature equating to $\frac{4}{8}$.

Mussorgsky	Gopak (from *Russian Masters*)	Schott

Like many other piano pieces of his, the Gopak (or Hopak) by Modeste Mussorgsky (1839–1881) is rough and energetic, ideal perhaps for the naturally heavy-handed — as if trying to live up (or down) to that famous portrait of him as a tousled, wild-eyed and red-nosed alcoholic (he did in fact drink himself to death). First impressions may mislead, however: much of the piece (in this edition, at least) is in fact **pp** or **p**, like the introductory imitation of a violin tuning up (notice that left hand changes chord over barline 10/11), and like the main theme — **p** at first (bar 18) even though **mf** later (bar 69) and with uncouth left-hand offbeat accents. This theme may sound familiar even if you've never seen the comic opera from which it comes (*The Fair at Sorochintsy*, composed 1874-1880), for it is often played alone as an orchestral item. The dance is big and energetic, but steady, *c.*♩ = 96–112. Hold bass notes where marked, either with fingers (bars 55–58) or pedal (18–21): pedal also the dotted crotchets in bars 35–41 to sustain them full length and avoid gaps over the barlines. The quintuplets and sextuplets in bars 43–47 of course go in strict time, as does the single empty bar (48). Guess the orchestration: lots of full orchestra with cymbals in the loud moments, say strings alone round barlines 59/60 and 61/62, then (a new colour for the new key) brass alone round 63/4 and 65/6; all *pizzicato* strings from 93 (so no pedal); brief clarinet solo in 96, flute in 100, piccolo in 101, and a **ppp** fade-out on glockenspiel or xylophone in 102.

| Chabrier | Danse villageoise, no. 7 of *10 Pièces Pittoresques* (from *Complete Works for Piano or* separately) | Dover *or* Enoch |

Unlike the introverted *Feuillet d'album* (see Grade 7), this Chabrier item is as energetic as his top hit *España*. It's a long but repetitive piece, and therefore easier to learn than at first glance. Check the bar-count (first-time bars are 46 and 141, second-time bars are 47 and 142), then note that bars 123/4–41 are more or less the same as 82/83–99, and 143–210 identical with 1–69. The main tune is earthy (village dance, not ballroom) but the phrasing subtle, with many 11-bar phrases (1–22, 48–69, 78–99) and one real mixture of 5, 4, 2 and 6-bar phrasings (bars 100–133).

Detach the vigorous opening theme (starting in A natural minor), with *pesante* quavers (same in the left hand later) to avoid rushing; compare opening f with the ff at 23, contrasting with briefly elegant p episode with twee trill (31–46) – the grace notes in bar 33 simply tie into the following chord. Imitate trombones in the left hand from 58/59, trumpet on top right-hand notes from 62/63, and bagpipe in open-fifths episode from 69/70 – then check Chabrier's own orchestration, which appears as the second movement of his *Suite pastorale*. Off-beat sf's in major-key section (from 78) may be dancers clapping hands, or playing tambourines, the *dolce legato* section from 117 a visit from the village beauty, gracing the dance floor with her presence before leaving it free again for the yokels with mud on their boots. Exploit the closing *allargando* (bar 209) to leave time for accurate octaves and an impressive finish.

Group B

| Grieg | Prelude from *From Holberg's Time* op. 40 | Trinity Guildhall |

Commonly known as the *Holberg Suite* and probably better known in its later version for string orchestra, this work bears the subtitle 'Suite in the Olden Style.' Ludvig Holberg (1684–1754) was a Danish-Norwegian poet, sometimes dubbed 'The Molière of the North', and Grieg wrote this deliberately antique-style suite as a bicentenary tribute. The toccata-style figuration may recall the Baroque era, but everyone's favourite moment, the crossed-hands tune starting at bar 9, is pure Grieg. Regular well-articulated and non-rushing semis are a first requirement, plus security in fast leaps (obviously so in bars 19 and 23 and even faster in bar 29), a large enough left hand (and/or good enough rotary arm action) to cope with the wide spreads of bars 42–43, and confidence enough to tackle bars 40–41 (quick arpeggiandos, fast scale and all) with minimal slowing down.

Keep the right hand relaxed during the continuous semiquaver movement, whether pattering or thunderous: some editions offer a brief respite by suggesting you take parts of bars 17–18 with RRLL. Hand-to-hand patterns are the obvious intention in bars 19–20 and 23–24: one fingering option, bizarre on paper but rewardingly forceful in performance, is to take most right-hand semis here with 3, while left hand goes 1 3 1 1/2 3 1 1 or whatever is convenient. Try placing R under L from bar 30, achieving a regular p pattering by fingering L 25 R 52; switch to R over L from bar 34's *più p*. Keep bar 42–45's melody joyous and lyrical as you wrestle with the left hand; the theme buried amid right-hand semis thereafter will form a warm duet with left-hand octaves. The *Coda* (from bar 68) is likewise lyrical, not just a succession of chords; the closing *rit.* is extremely grand and can make the piece close more than three times slower than it began. Place the final octave G grace note as a demisemi before the beat, i.e. at the very end of the previous bar.

| Elgar | In Smyrna | Trinity Guildhall |

Elgar is rarely, if ever, thought of as a composer for piano, and *In Smyrna* is probably the best of his solo pieces. It dates from 1905 (the year of the *Introduction and Allegro* for strings) and was inspired by a Mediterranean cruise (Smyrna being the Western European name for Izmir, in Turkey). You might imagine a gentle bow wave – or the rhythmic purr of ship's engines – in the right-hand semiquavers, while the expressive tenor line floats freely beneath, encouraged by quiet drum taps in the bass, all carefully balanced with three different dynamic markings: yes, bar 3's drum taps may be *pp* like bar 5's, even though not marked thus by Elgar. Some four-against-three rhythms in fact look harder than they are: mathematical exactitude is not a requirement given the prevailing *rubato*, and in the first bars of what might be called each verse (bars 2 and 12), simply take care to desynchronise the final notes in each hand. Bars 23-25 are undeniably trickier, not just because semis switch (quietly, without bumps) from hand to hand but because excessive *rubato* here may impede the flow.

Despite the G major mode, there is great melancholy here – Elgar had been ill for much of the year – and once away from the opening theme his moods change without warning. Bar 8 is already a warm *f* (chords just beneath the tenor melody are taken with right hand, in case you were wondering: the left hand plays bass octaves and crossed-over treble clef chords in bars 8-9), yet its reprise at bar 15 is *pp*. Notice the flattened leading-note in each case. No two bars of the new theme in sixths (imagine muted violins, and/or two clarinets) are the same dynamic or tempo: compare bar 18 (*stringendo*) with equivalent bars 26 (*rit.*) and 30 (*a tempo, più lento*). Compare second beats of bar 23 (D♮ in both hands) with 25 (sharps, the left hand sharpened from the grace note onwards) and 29 (where the original A♯ is also replaced by less colourful A♮). Bar 41 looks as big-textured as bar 39, but is now *p* rather than *ff*. Start the cadenza at roughly ♪ = ♪ and, as with all such small-note cadenzas, respect the chosen relative note values even if not 100% mathematically. Check the four cadenza quavers before bar 44: B♭, C♯, E♮ (with compulsory pause), G (ditto): then start counting a careful eight quavers, noticing that what were originally semis are now demis, and therefore start after (rather than on) the counts of four and eight.

| Piazzolla | Street Tango | Trinity Guildhall |

Argentinian composer Astor Piazzolla was a student of compatriot Alberto Ginastera, and also of Nadia Boulanger (see sister Lili, among this Grade's alternative pieces). He was, in the words of guitarist John Duarte, 'a man with a mission: to establish the tango and the milonga ... as art forms.' Of these two dances, the milonga did not reach Europe, but the tango did, becoming immensely popular. Piazzolla was almost unknown here before the 1980s but has achieved a cult following since: his harmonies may seem crude and his melodies unoriginal, but there is unvarnished passion in his music, and the atmosphere he creates is that of the sweat, perfume, cigarette smoke and raucous applause of a cramped tango bar in downtown Buenos Aires. Imagine the sound of an accordion (strictly speaking bandoneon) throughout, with the characteristic heavy tread of non-*staccato* bass notes. Bar 23's footnote about *rubato* is vital: Piazzolla himself used to play this kind of theme so freely that any truly accurate notation would be thick with syncopations and irregular (partly tied-over) quintuplets, sextuplets and so on.

Change the mood as much as the text allows, from bar 30: a lightened left hand will help. From bar 39 the arpeggiandos continue *simile*, as suggested: so do the accents. Count carefully into bar 52 (a non-*rubato* moment) to avoid slipping into left-hand triplets, as their grouping on the page tempts you to do. The closing tremolo (bars 104–105) is exciting, even more so if pedalled: the excitement will have been enhanced if you have reached molto *f* by bar 103, the culmination of a very long *crescendo*.

Françaix	Little Upstart	
	(no. 10 of *Ten Pieces for Children to Play and Dream*)	Trinity Guildhall

Like the whole album from which this piece is taken, much of Jean Françaix's music was written for children – and even when writing for grown-ups there is a general innocence and lightness about his sound-world that makes you fear than if you let go the sheet music, it would not fall to the floor but float towards the ceiling. Like Piazzolla, he was a Nadia Boulanger student, learning (or inheriting) from her a sense of elegance and well-mannered craftsmanship: his *Piano Concertino* is much admired and is technically not at all difficult.

The hero of this *Little Upstart* surely works in the circus, possibly as a clown: his polka has more than a few red-nose moments like the sudden crash in bar 4, the faint trombone *glissando* octaves in bars 14/15–19, carefully fingered to slide off black keys onto white, and the Prokofievian side-slips in and out of key (bars 31–32 and from 39–40). Finish the whole piece with absolutely no *rit.* or holding-on of the last chord, for the ending should take listeners completely by surprise. Take a steady tempo, not through fear of black-looking bars 12 and 28 (which are nothing more than Ab major scales) but simply to make bar 25 rhythmically intelligible. Contrast right-hand *staccato* with *legatissimo* left hand in bars 9–11; compare different articulations and dynamics between bars 29–32 and 37–40. Yes, bar 48 really does end on a chord containing Ab and A# (and D♮, still) – and no, the few printed pedal markings do not imply you can't pedal elsewhere: bars like 12 and 28 positively benefit from it.

Takemitsu	Litany (*in Memory of Michael Vyner*)	Trinity Guildhall

Japanese composer Toru Takemitsu is best-known for his orchestral music which occasionally incorporates Japanese instruments like the biwa and shakuhachi, and even without them inhabits a lush, relaxed and near-timeless Oriental world that musically also recalls Debussy, Messiaen and early Schoenberg. It is surprising, therefore, to learn that he was originally very unconventional, experimenting with musique concrète, free improvisation, graphic notation and aleatorism. His stated aim was 'to give a proper meaning to the 'streams of sounds' which penetrate the world that surrounds us.' Like countless other contemporary composers, Takemitsu was deeply grateful to dedicatee Michael Vyner, who, as artistic director of the London Sinfonietta, gave priceless opportunities to get their works performed.

There's a detectable Japanese accent to Takemitsu's *Litany*, partly through a prevailing chord of ascending C-Db-F-G. As an experiment, try quickly arpeggiating and sustaining it: then see it used in bar 1, the bass of bars 8–9 and the theme in bars 17–18.

Rhythms look tough on paper but the piece moves very slowly, providing plenty of time to negotiate the numerous changes of register and texture as well as count odd-looking rhythms like that in bar 8 (and similar bar 13), where the chord comes after one quaver's-worth of bass note, the bass resuming one semiquaver later. Strike a balance between the carefully notated rhythms and the initial instruction *con rubato*. When printed, such multi-layered music often forces notes out of position on the page: treble Db and B♮ come together with left-hand Bb on the third beat of bar 5 (and transposed equivalent bar 30), while Bb and B♮ sound simultaneously with G to start bar 11. Don't overlook bar 9's final bass note as the left hand skips around. Odd time signatures in bars 41 and 43 read 'three-point-five four', i.e. $\frac{7}{8}$.

Subtleties of pedalling are carefully marked, and require equally careful practice so that half-caught slowly-released piano strings (as in bar 18) don't go 'miaow!' – this is risky on a strange piano, so practice before the exam on as many different instruments as possible. The closing pedals are simpler, some being notated, like Debussy's, with tied notes you can't hold with fingers (bars 41 and 44). Others are marked with French ties, implying some sustaining beyond the written duration: try pedalling the start of bars 42 and 45, releasing just after (not exactly on) finger-held dotted crotchet chord. The blurred start to this chord not only respects the previous French tie but also helps to convey the (strictly speaking impossible) printed *cresc.* and *dim.* Make sure that bar 45's middle-register chord is firmly caught and continues to resound through bars 46 and 47.

| Chaminade | Pierrette op. 41 (from *Female Composers*) | Schott |

French pianist Cécile Chaminade composed over 200 pieces for her instrument. They include a sonata and two trios, but she is best known for smaller works like the lush and once-popular concert study *Automne*. She wrote in an old-fashioned style for her time (1857-1944) that recalls Mendelssohn, Schumann or Grieg, leading some reference books to patronise her compositions – but they are all charming, and rewarding to play. Technically, *Pierrette* contains some hand-crossing and many wide skips, most of them needing to land gently though not the extravagant leaps from bars 107 and 115: these, plus the subtitle 'Air de Ballet' (i.e. danceable) and the marking of 'Allegretto' rather than *Allegro* (i.e. steady, not fast) should dictate the chosen tempo. The piece looks dauntingly long for slow learners perhaps, but it is very repetitive, and bars 84-106 actually repeat bars 35-57 exactly, save for a final hand-crossed and easily overlooked Ab (formerly Bb).

To a modern editor, the printed pedal marks look debatable and incomplete: bar 31's could possibly lift a quaver earlier (bar 1's could match it, as could bars 3 and 33) while those in bars 60, 62, 68 and 70 could extend to the end of the minim, which would otherwise be cut short: yet if the nearby *mf*s are advanced by a quaver (which is where the new phrases really start) then the printed pedallings would make more sense. The overall intention is clear, however – and let your ears be the final judges. Notice the louder restart and *dim.* in bars 31-32: conversely, treat bar 64's *pp leggierissimo* with the awareness that a *ppp* is still to come. Preserve strict time through bars 29-30: and if unable to stretch the tenths in bars 42 and 44, try placing the grace note on (not before) the beat and catch it with pedal before you let go. The overall rhythm in possibly hard-to-read bars 123-124 is quaver-two-semis. Add colour throughout by carefully observing the (sometimes extreme) changes of dynamics.

| Debussy | Dr Gradus ad Parnassum (from *Children's Corner*) | Wiener Urtext *or* Alfred |

Children's Corner contains the famous *Golliwogg's Cakewalk*, but the humour in *Dr Gradus* is more subtle, starting in the title which pokes fun at piano practice via Clementi's book of studies with the same title (and musically, recalling Heller's *The Brook* – see Grade 7). Neat well-practised fingerwork is essential for the joke, with no pedal until bar 5 (suggested there by the melody's change from *staccato* quavers to crotchets) – from bar 7 Debussy (typically) indicates his pedal requirements not with the usual markings but by long notes impossible to sustain with fingers alone. Bar 11 may be pedalled with four crotchets (and the extended equivalent bars 55-56 with semibreve then four crotchets), then try using no pedal until bar 24, where – as in bars 33-34 and 37-38 – half-changing on new harmonies may preserve the bass without blurring the treble: middle pedal catching low bass is another option here, but strictly for the very confident.

Compare bars 7 and 9 (*cresc./dim.*) with 8 and 10 (none – and different descending right-hand notes); compare dots and *tenuto* dashes in 17 and 19; make 33-36 dreamy and from 37 only gradually more exciting. Try bars 57-64 LRRR rather than the printed LLRR in order to emphasise the trumpet-theme more; compare alternate *dim*s and *cresc*s in 65-66; play the right-hand Bs very hard in 67 and 69 to complete the middle-register theme, and end very vigorously with possibly no *rall*.

Joplin	Gladiolus Rag (from *Piano Rags* book 1)	Schott

'Do not play this piece fast,' Scott Joplin himself warned us, 'It is never right to play Ragtime fast' – so all those show-off friends who rattle through *Maple Leaf Rag* at 100mph are in fact wrong. The correct speed for *Gladiolus* (*Slow march tempo*, notice) will turn bars 20-24 (left hand) and 49-50 (right hand) from something unattainable into quite easy octaves (though if you can barely stretch an octave at all, then choose elsewhere). All the same, make periodic checks with a metronome, to resist the temptation to hurry in the easy bits.

Players already knowing *Maple Leaf* (probably most of us) – in its original key of A♭, that is – may risk drifting into it by accident if playing *Gladiolus* from memory, for the very same harmonies recur, strikingly so from bar 9 and through 16-19. The 'B' section (from bar 48/49) is even in the same key as *Maple Leaf*'s, and both rags close thereafter in this second key without making a *D.C.*. End the piece loudly and convincingly, then, so that the audience realises there is no mistake. In this generally straightforward harmony, don't overlook F♭ on the third quaver of bar 55, particularly as an incorrect F♮ would sound 'right' – and carefully move to left-hand A♭ halfway through bar 77: tempting to play A♮ instead, straight after those sound-alike B double flats. The mood is mostly calm, the *f* second section (from bar 17) being brighter without aggression, and the big-looking piano concerto stuff (from bar 49) actually marked quieter than anything else. Aim to bring out the right-hand thumb melody from bar 65, adding liveliness (without rushing) by closing each two-bar phrase (bars 66, 68, 70, 74, etc.) with a pair of *staccato* quaver chords.

Rachmaninov	Mélodie op. 3 no. 3	
	(from *Rachmaninoff Piano Compositions* vol. 3)	Boosey & Hawkes

This dreamy 'song without words' is from the same set as Rachmaninov's famous C♯ minor Prelude. It needs the ability to spin out (and shape) a connected *cantabile* line at a very slow tempo whilst balancing rich accompaniments discreetly in the background: bar 17/18, for instance, proceeds at three different dynamics simultaneously. It needs confidence with three-against-twos, some more clearly notated than others: third beat of bar 14, for instance, is three-against-two but the fourth beat, though similarly aligned on the page, is not – and the ends of bars 10-11 should be counted as duplets against silent triplets to avoid rushing. Finally, the piece needs an awareness of suitable *rubato*

– lingering over extra-juicy chords, and pushing forward in exciting moments – for although a good starting tempo is ♩ = 52, it could advance to around 66 from bar 18 (the bit that recalls John Field's 5th Nocturne) and ♩ = 76 from bar 26.

Lavish pedalling is *de rigueur*, regardless of any printed rests between triplets: start with a whole-bar pedal, therefore, and repedal only when chords and/or melody notes change (e.g. on first three beats of bar 5). Big-looking bar 32 is actually pp, though a full-orchestral f is not long in coming (bar 36), followed by stately scales on trumpets and trombones (36/37) and a dramatic tuba solo (bar 38). Count bar 39 carefully to avoid inadvertently doubling the speed, however fast you may have got: *rall.* as you count through bar 40 so as seamlessly to regain Tempo I at bar 41. If the printed layout is uncomfortable, try swapping hands from here through to the fourth beat of bar 49, placing melody in the left hand and triplets in the right: this makes it easier to land gently on the bass notes (which should be one notch softer, as was bar 18, and as bar 50 should be). Rhythms from here are mostly smoothed into the prevailing triplet pulse, though watch for isolated offbeat duplets in bar 45 and from bar 53. Repedal cleanly to start slow-cadenza bar 59, carefully notated in small semibreves rather than quavers and which may themselves slow down as you approach the final G# (not an E!).

Ireland	Month's Mind from *London Pieces* (from *Collected Piano Works* vol. 4)	Stainer & Bell

This is among the best small pieces by John Ireland (1879-1962, and English despite his surname), as good as *April* and *The Darkened Valley* and much deeper than *The Island Spell*. The mood is pastoral, intimate and nostalgic, with brief bursts of flaring anguish; the harmony is rich, prompting not just careful sight reading but a feeling for *rubato* that instinctively lingers over subtle chord changes and pushes on through the urgent moments. The title is fully explained in the printed copy, but briefly means 'a longing desire'.

Many subtleties of composition lie in wait: the repeating phrase from bar 21, successively compressed from nine crotchets to eight then six, each one louder than the last; the five-plus-one-bar phrases from bar 44 in an irregular mix of $\frac{2}{4}$ and $\frac{3}{4}$ time (hence the double time signature); the ever-higher-rising decoration as bars 50–51's phrase repeats; the three-note motto of the opening, recurring in a remote key at bar 34 and recapitulated in a weaker key (a tone lower) than expected (bar 69), with a subversive chromatically altered bass line, and compressed by omitting the equivalent of bar 7. This weaker key drags the music down at bar 78, shaken off by a compensating higher-rising sequence inserted at bar 84 and peaceably regaining its original key in a more delicate upper register from bar 99. Near-continuous though sensitive pedalling is required: French ties (from notes into rests) in bars 61 and 63 imply long pedals (two bars at a time, possibly releasing as the background murmur emerges into a melody one beat before 65) and may be pencilled into bars 95 and 97 where the intention is surely the same.

Bridge	Valse Capricieuse (from *Three Sketches*)	Boosey & Hawkes

Frank Bridge's best-known piano piece is *Rosemary*, the previous item in this set; his best-known orchestral piece is *The Sea* – and his best-known composition student was Benjamin Britten. This waltz (1906) is full of Edwardian whimsy with gowns, long dresses and fluttering shawls, and demands some instinct for *rubato* – a basic general pulse should prevail but metronomic exactness is to be avoided. The suggested marking (♩ = 80) can sound hectic if not perfectly controlled: ♩ = 63 may better suit the markings *moderato* and *grazioso* and leave room for a faster closing *Presto*. In any event, try starting under tempo, reaching basic speed in bars 2–4, then *accel.* through bar 5, *poco rall.* in 8, *allargando* in passionate bar 13 and *calmando* at 16. Breathe for a moment on the double barline, play quick grace notes for excitement in 18–19; broaden a little for big sound in the tricky right hand of bars 21–23 (finger these 14 25 13 24 35 25/14 2 1 5 4 1/1 2 1 5 4 2). Notice the changed note amid left-hand ties over barline 25/26; *accel.* through 27–28 without jeopardising 29 (finger right hand 1 2 4 1 2 4/5 4 2 1 4 2/1 2 13 5 14 2 and sustain the full-toned left-hand harmony). Bars 31–42 are 17–28 transposed; sustain the right hand of 44 without pedal to contrast with the *staccato* left.

The passion of bar 13 returns at 57, and increases by semitones at 61 and 65 (make each key change *più f*): *accel.* as much as possible in 66–68 without losing control. Pedal the last two quavers of 70 (unmarked, though probably by accident) exactly as the previous four. If the left hand is too small to sustain bars 71–78 unpedalled, and if blurred chromatics fail to appeal, then pedal 71 (and 75), release thumb, soundlessly regain the lower three notes, then change harmony in 74 (and 78) without losing the bass. The closing *accel.* (with long, short or no pedal – you choose) persists through the last two throwaway chords.

Bartók	Rondo no. 1 (from *3 Rondos on Folk Tunes*)	Universal

No. 1 is by far the most tuneful of the Three Rondos, and may inspire nervous listeners to explore Bartók further. Apart from tricky bars 103–118 and hard-to-balance 139–146, it is quite straightforward for players with reliable rhythm, and well suits small hands. Check the bar count: empty bars are all numbered (87–88 and 92–94) and notated like bars' rest in orchestral parts.

Phrase the opening innocently, like a nursery rhyme, bringing off left-hand chords punctually and making the left louder than the right at bar 16 to finish the phrase audibly. Shatter the mood with sudden *ff* at bar 24 after silence (the pause); check soprano/tenor articulation over sustained alto/bass harmony from bar 36. New metronome markings at bars 44 and 55 are increases in speed – a kindly composer might have added *più mosso* each time to save you checking back or memorising the previous marking. *Ossia*s from bars 57 and 69 can be disregarded. Count the bars' rest precisely (check with a metronome) and resume the mood of innocence at bar 95 with a big yawn at 101 (note sudden *mf* and the word *molto*). Try practising the *Allegro giocoso* with separate hands, fingering the right hand of bar 111 with 3 124 3 124 to ensure lifts after slurs, and crushing all left-hand grace notes very close to avoid rhythmic distortion.

Bring out top right-hand notes from bar 131 to maximise contrast with the trickier requirement from 139, where thumb notes can be made louder than others by changing forearm position: either twist outwards so that the thumb strikes faster (from higher up), or (conversely) twist inwards and press thumb hard. Different methods suit different players. Each slur in 147–148 may be pedalled; save the most tender playing of all for the final nursery rhyme phrase (152–161), carefully replaying the last top C (bar 161) while tying the lower voices – so they all live happily ever after.

Bowen	Shadows (from *2 Preludes* op. 100)	Weinberger

English composer, pianist and teacher York Bowen (born Edwin Yorke Bowen, 1884, died 1961) is best known today for his solo piano pieces, though he also wrote four piano concertos and one each for violin and viola, plus two symphonies and many fine duo sonatas. *Shadows* is currently paired with an untitled G minor work but was originally meant to share its opus number (100) with '*Ripples* – a short sketch'. Time signature and tempo marking for *Shadows* seem to have disappeared (the previous piece was headed 'Andante sostenuto') – it may go as a very slow alla breve (try ♩ = 46, i.e. ♩ = 92). The opening mood recalls Bax's *Country Tune* while there is some unashamed Rachmaninov passion later on (bars 32–35, with whole-bar pedalling, and quieter 50–51, each with dotted minim-crotchet pedals): technical requirements are smooth left-hand arpeggios, well-voiced *cantabile* right-hand chords, and careful pedalling, particularly at the opening, to strike a balance between sustained chords and non-blurred partly chromatic low-register quavers.

The first right-hand F♯ may be sustained as a minim for harmonic richness as quavers proceed; minim and quaver D are simultaneous despite their printed non-alignment; bars 14 and 52 contain C♯, not natural; *rubato* in bar 16 helps to close the first paragraph, in preparation for bar 18/19's fresh start. Bar 55 is reflective but need not *rit.* prematurely; don't repedal for the very last low D.

Boulanger	D'un vieux jardin (from *Female Composers*)	Schott

Two sisters, two contrasting fortunes: Nadia Boulanger died in 1979 aged 92 after a career as an internationally renowned teacher, numbering among her students Aaron Copland, Elliott Carter, Walter Piston, Lennox Berkeley – and Grade 8 album contributors Astor Piazzolla and Jean Françaix. Lili's composing career, on the other hand, was plagued by constant ill-health and she died at the age of only 25. She was prolific all the same: her best big piece is probably the psalm-setting *Du fond de l'Abîme*, and she was the first woman composer ever to win the Prix de Rome (1913).

D'un vieux jardin, composed in 1914, is introspective but infinitely subtle, tonal but very chromatic, largely gloomy but with sunlit moments. It needs flexible *rubato* (from around ♩ = 69), big hands (even though spread chords and/or pedal can often help) and a keen eye for accidentals: the only non-inflected notes in bars 5–6, for instance, are all flats apart from one C, and everyone misses the unmarked E♮ (not flat) that closes bar 10 and swings the music back to its opening C sharp minor. Check the voice-leading in bar 2, whose final F♮ brings in an overlapping fresh voice: this pattern recurs, thickened out, in bar 33, and with ever more intensity in bar 35, the only *ff* in the piece. Sustain out-of-reach bass in bars like 16–17 by fingering the chords 5212 and securely catching low F♮s with pedal. Bars 23–25 may remind you of Fauré, a close personal friend of the sisters; bars 28–32 sound like five attempts to recall the chord with which the whole piece started. Replay bar 15's A♭ then hold for the rest of the bar; try taking bar 31's downbeat G♮ and upper B in right hand (pedal will cover) similarly bar 36's high left hand G♮ and A. Grace notes to bars 32, 42 and so on are extremely leisurely, going well before the beat. *Rall.* towards bar 49's *très lent* triplet, counting three per beat both before and after so as not to distort the overall rhythm however slowly you choose to finish.

Confrey — Dizzy Fingers [with repeats] — Alfred

Flashy, easy, appealing and unremittingly light-hearted, this will suit many candidates – and most listeners – though thoughtful ones may get tired of it before long. 'Zez', if you were wondering, stood not for Zebedee or Ezekiel, but Elzear, Edward Confrey's real second name. Born 1895 in Peru Illinois, into a musical family that included an elder brother who could play seven instruments, Zez was picking out tunes on the piano at the age of four. His adult career included dance and jazz bands: he composed steadily until after World War II, whereupon he retired, living until 1971. His first hit was *Kitten on the Keys* (1921), closely followed by *Dizzy Fingers* and *Stumblin'*, among others. His immensely successful *Modern Course in Novelty Piano Playing* appeared in 1923 and remained in print for over 40 years, being advertised thus: 'Modern Piano playing is full of Tricks' and promising to teach you all the 'Tricks' with which to dazzle everyone within earshot.

Tell your serious-minded friends that this is actually a rondo, with two episodes in different keys. Quick arpeggios on chords A^6 and B^9, and scales of E and A major, form the bulk of the technical challenge, and you have several chances to get them right. Don't overlook the stepwise bass in bar 6 (and whenever it recurs), a rare departure from tonic and dominant; try changing bar 38's suggested 4th finger to another 3rd for extra power on the accent; highlight the three-beat right-hand syncopations (another 'Trick') from bar 101 – and if your edition has chord symbols, change bar 113's G to a D ^{sus4}. The most effective Trick of all is to avoid rushing (try recording yourself and check your opening and closing speeds with a metronome) – and stay in control, to avoid any bad jokes about Butter Fingers!

Kapustin — Sonatina op. 100 — A-RAM. Moscow

Almost totally unknown until a few years ago, Nikolai Kapustin (born Ukraine, 1937) made a career as a jazz pianist – enterprisingly so, in a Communist regime, but easily guessable from almost every bar of his copious piano output. It all sounds like Oscar Peterson, or Burt Bacharach, or Bill Evans … dazzling to listen to, but with only two exceptions all fearfully difficult to play. One exception is the Toccatina op. 36, the other is this one-movement Sonatina, the kind of jazz homage to classical style that Joseph Horovitz has also explored.

It proceeds like the first movement of a Haydn sonata, all quavers being straight, not swung. It requires controlled neatness of phrasing and unexaggerated dynamics despite all the blue notes and syncopations, and classically-phrased question-and-answer treatment in bars 9-12. Bar 15 contains straight quavers (no triplets, despite the grouping of tails) which may be fingered (right hand) 25 1 5/14 5 1 2 3 5 321 around barline 15/16. Distinguish between ♩♪ and ♪♪♩ in bars 16, 18 and 20-28; lift the left hand very high in 22 to let the right in, and finger the right hand in bars 24/5/6 with 34 2 1/25 3 2 34 2 1/34 (take A's here with the left). Accent simultaneous fifth fingers in crossed-hands bar 31 for best coordination, and keep steady in rush-prone bars 33-36.

Check the bar count: we number second-time bars as 45-46, and the pause bar as 61. The opening theme, previously detached, is slurred in the left hand in bars 49, 53 and 56. Leave E unaccompanied in 61; resist lingering in bar 63 (already Tempo I). Left-hand G♯ persists through bar 79; after 82's quaver rest, finger the right hand with 45–slide–45 12. Written-out right-hand 'fills' in 94-95 may be fingered 12 125 1 3 45 214/314 314 321 LLL, and in 99/100/101 (G♮s have been omitted here: 99 and 101 should match 100) 234 23 23/21 234 24 23/21. The left hand in 104 may start 12 3 1 5; the whole movement ends with a possible *cresc.* and definitely no *rit*.